The New York Times

IN THE HEADLINES

Doping

THE SPORTS WORLD IN CRISIS

EDUCATIONAL PUBLISHING
BOOKS

THE NEW YORK TIMES EDITORIAL STAFF

Published in 2019 by The New York Times® Educational Publishing in association with The Rosen Publishing Group, Inc.
29 East 21st Street, New York, NY 10010

First Edition

The New York Times
Alex Ward: Editorial Director, Book Development
Phyllis Collazo: Photo Rights/Permissions Editor
Heidi Giovine: Administrative Manager

Rosen Publishing
Megan Kellerman: Managing Editor
Xina M. Uhl: Editor
Greg Tucker: Creative Director
Brian Garvey: Art Director

Cataloging-in-Publication Data
Names: New York Times Company.
Title: Doping: the sports world in crisis / edited by the New York Times editorial staff.
Description: New York : New York Times Educational Publishing, 2019. | Series: In the headlines | Includes glossary and index.
Identifiers: ISBN 9781642821161 (library bound) | ISBN 9781642821147 (pbk.) | ISBN 9781642821154 (ebook)
Subjects: LCSH: Doping in sports—Juvenile literature. | Athletes—Drug use—Juvenile literature.
Classification: LCC RC1230.D677 2019 | DDC 362.29'088796—dc23

Manufactured in the United States of America

On the cover: The use of performance-enhancing substances is banned in sports, but doping continues to be an issue; MirageC/Moment Open/Getty Images.

Contents

CHAPTER 3

Bucking the System

CHAPTER 4

The Bigger They Are, the Harder They Fall

CHAPTER 5

Falling Through the Cracks

CHAPTER 6

Antidoping and the Future

Introduction

AS LONG AS SPORTS competitions have existed, there has been the temptation for the athletes and those associated with them — coaches, trainers, doctors and others — to cheat. In the modern era one form of cheating is called doping, which involves the use of illegal substances or methods to make athletes perform better. It can also refer to attempts to tamper with doping controls and refusing to take drug tests.

There are five different classes of banned drugs. Stimulants and hormones are the most common. These drugs are effective at enhancing performance. However, they also have negative physical effects. Stimulants increase athletes' blood flow and heart rate to make them more alert and to diminish exhaustion, but they can also cause heart failure and addiction.

Athletes may make use of masking agents and diuretics to hide drug use by removing fluid from the body. Cannabinoids and narcotic analgesics are used for pain, but they are addictive and can make injuries worse. Glucocorticoids are anti-inflammatories that cover up serious injuries.

Anabolic steroids give athletes the ability to build muscle and train harder. They can be administered orally in tablet form, injected into the muscles or applied to the skin in gels or creams. Side effects involve aggression and kidney damage. Less serious side effects include low sperm count and baldness for men and deepened voices and increased facial hair for women.

Peptide hormones increase muscle mass and strength. These substances give athletes more energy by increasing red blood cells. Beta blockers are used to lower the heart rate and keep hands from trembling in sports such as shooting and archery.

TIM DE WAELE/VELO/GETTY IMAGES

Lance Armstrong celebrates his Tour de France victory in 1999. His seven consecutive wins were voided in 2012 after his use of performance-enhancing drugs was discovered.

Blood doping involves removing athletes' blood and increasing their oxygen levels by injecting it back into their bodies. This practice can result in heart failure and kidney failure.

Despite the dangers of these substances, athletes, coaches, sports organizations and others have made liberal use of them. The desire to win at all costs is potent motivation for such actions. Organizations such as the World Anti-Doping Agency (WADA) work toward ensuring that sports worldwide are free of doping. In the United States, the U.S. Anti-Doping Agency (USADA) functions as the national anti-doping organization for the Olympics, Paralympics and other sports.

This collection of articles looks at the issue of doping in sports from different angles. Chapter 1 traces early problems with the doping of racing animals and in the Olympics and the move toward regulation of substances that enhance performance. Chapter 2 explores the issues encountered as antidoping laws were put into place as well as the effects of various performance-enhancing drugs. Chapter 3 focuses on doping fraud committed by individuals and organizations and on dissenting views about antidoping efforts. Chapter 4 looks at a number of high-profile doping scandals in cycling, baseball and the Olympics. Chapter 5 covers problems with doping regulations, from the possibility of competitors sabotaging athletes to issues with a lack of valid data and resistance of certain organizations to following antidoping standards. Chapter 6 involves advances in pharmacology, lawmaking about performance-enhancing drugs and continuing attempts to fool the antidoping systems.

The sports world continues to make headlines as individuals and organizations alike navigate competing pressures to succeed in high stakes events and to also follow antidoping regulations. With legal and ethical issues at play, the controversy of doping is multi-faceted and demands careful reporting.

CHAPTER 1

Problems and Protections

Money played a big role in athletic competitions in the early 20th century, especially when it came to races by dogs and horses. Racing promoters didn't hesitate to use drugs to enhance the performance of racing animals, making it necessary to create laws to limit such fraudulent behavior. Olympic athletes, coaches and promoters often gave in to the temptation to use performance-enhancing drugs as well. The establishment of testing procedures took decades to implement, and even then they were not always effective.

U.S. Orders State Racing Bodies to Eliminate 'Doping' of Horses

BY THE NEW YORK TIMES | MARCH 29, 1936

WASHINGTON, MARCH 28 — America's reputed $500,000,000 race-horse business is under the close scrutiny of the Federal Government in connection with the nation-wide drive against the use of narcotics to stimulate or depress the running ability of the animals.

As the horses were about to go to the barriers in many Spring meets, Harry J. Anslinger, chief of the Federal Bureau of Narcotics, announced that the State Racing Commissions would have one more opportunity to "clean up their own back yards," but that if they failed, drastic Federal action would follow.

The tentative draft of a law already has been prepared by the

Treasury to prohibit the interstate shipment of drugged horses for racing purposes and to deny track licenses to persons guilty of this practice.

The draft is regulatory in nature, based on the principle of the Securities Act, to prevent frauds against the public. The proposed law will be held in abeyance and will be introduced only if the State commissions fail to eliminate or properly regulate the "hopping" of horses.

Mr. Anslinger is determined to see that horse "hopping" is successfully outlawed. He said today that while the Narcotic Bureau does not have the agents actually to patrol the tracks, except in emergency cases, the Federal Government will prosecute under the Harrison Anti-Narcotic Law all cases of importance reported by the State commissions.

The State commissions, following a meeting of the National Association of State Racing Commissioners in Florida in January, pledged support to a clean-up campaign against the horse "fixers." This drive was begun three years ago when the practice of injecting narcotics into racehorses, thoroughbred and otherwise, to increase their speed, was general.

Mr. Anslinger expressed the opinion today that "doping" had been reduced greatly in all States which have racing commissions, although no such progress has been made in the United States as in Canada, where racing has been placed on a remarkably purified basis from this standpoint.

The principal racing States are New York, Florida, Kentucky, Maryland, Rhode Island, New Hampshire, Massachusetts, Ohio, Michigan, Arkansas, California, Illinois, Washington, West Virginia, Texas and Louisiana. In the opinion of Federal officials the most effective racing regulations are those of New York and Florida, although other States were described as doing an "excellent job" in their clean-up operations.

Mr. Anslinger and Dr. H. J. Wollner, consulting chemist to Secretary Morgenthau, were observers at the Florida meeting. They particularly approved a plan to set up a national committee on which would be represented horsemen, State commissions and the Federal Government. This organization, now in the process of formation, will make continuing studies of the narcotic situation and "keep abreast of the times."

WILL TEST ALL WINNERS

Another important decision, heartily approved by Mr. Anslinger, was the determination to make saliva tests of all winners. By the saliva test it can be determined whether a horse has been drugged. Heretofore it has been the customary practice to test only two winners out of the conventional seven races. Usually the seventh race finds "doped" horses, because ordinarily the two tests are made in the earlier events.

Mr. Anslinger also saw a serious and growing evil in the "doping" of favorites or even-money horses to prevent their winning races. Gangs betting against the favorites are held to be depressing horses with narcotics. Careful inquiries and laboratory investigations are being made by the State commissions and the Federal authorities to determine what narcotics are being used.

The entire "horse-hopping" question is under scientific observation at Temple University, the Brooklyn Polytechnic Institute, Ohio State University, the University of Pennsylvania and government and State official laboratories.

Dogs 'Doped' in Britain

BY CABLE TO THE NEW YORK TIMES | FEB. 29, 1944

LONDON, FEB. 28 — Recent outbreaks of "doping" of racing dogs in various parts of England by racketeers have resulted in special details of police and private guards being posted at the dog tracks, especially in the north of England.

Dog racing, which in recent years has attracted crowds rivaling those attending horse races, is a popular sport in this country and betting at them is lively.

Doping Tests Urged for All Harness Horses Before Races at State Tracks

BY DEANE MCGOWEN | NOV. 13, 1959

THE STANDARDBRED OWNERS ASSOCIATION yesterday proposed pre-race testing of all harness horses competing at the eight tracks in New York State.

The association said the move was designed to insure that racing was conducted as honestly as possible, thereby protecting the betting public. The association also hopes it will halt careless talk about doped trotters and pacers and questionable racing.

Such talk has been prevalent during the Roosevelt Raceway meeting at Westbury, L. I. However, unsubstantiated charges also are directed at other tracks.

Jesse Moss, counsel for the association, and Woody Lawlis, executive director, submitted the proposal at a meeting with the press at the Hotel Manhattan.

MOSS ADVOCATES PLAN

"The association is strongly in favor of pre-race testing as the only suitable thing to correct the present situation," Moss said.

"Until now the S. O. A. has been content to follow the lead of both the track owners and the State Harness Racing Commission as to the conduct of the racing, the rules and the security measures.

"However, the recent allegations have made it necessary for the horsemen to take some action since it is their livelihood which is being affected.

"So from now on the association's voice will be heard strongly in order to promote the best interests of harness racing and protect the betting public."

STAGGERED TESTS PROPOSED

The association proposed that each horse competing at state tracks be placed in a receiving barn three hours before it races. All the horses would not be placed in the receiving barn simultaneously. The tests would be staggered throughout the late afternoon and early evening.

It was proposed that a testing machine, known as the spectrophotometer, be purchased to analyze urine samples of the horses for indications of such drugs as procaine or ephedrin. The spokesmen said that the method was not perfect, but that it could produce evidence of drugs in most cases.

Moss said the tests could be completed within two hours and if any evidence of drugs was found the horse would be scratched. He said the horsemen were in favor of the proposal.

The machine costs about $8,000, Moss said. However, such items as the operation of the receiving barn and increased security personnel would bring the overall cost closer to $10,000, he pointed out.

The association believes the state and the harness tracks should share the expense of the machine and the other expenses involved, Moss said. He urged the State Commission to apply to the State Legislature for the necessary funds as well as for an additional law making pre-race testing mandatory.

Moss criticized the State attitude toward the sport as one of "policemen and tax collectors." He maintained the policing was not sufficiently in the public interest. He said the association was interested in preventive methods of policing, not simply in post-race policing. At present post-race examinations of the money finishers of each race are held.

The association also is studying ways of obtaining quicker and more just treatment for drivers accused of rules infractions. At present, Moss said, a driver may be suspended for as long as ten days before he gets a hearing. Then the hearing is held and the judgment is upheld by the commission, he charged. "This is execution before trial and is totally unjust to the driver and to the public," Moss said.

The procedure puts a tremendous burden upon the commissioners, he pointed out. He said they scarcely can be expected, eight or ten days later, to rule against the judge or judges who first spotted the infraction and ordered the suspension.

Moss indicated the association would propose a hearing within thirty-six hours for a suspect driver.

Use of Drugs at Olympics Found to Be Widespread

BY NEIL AMDUR | NOV. 10, 1972

DESPITE ELABORATE DOPING control procedures, the use and availability of drugs at the recent Olympics appear to have been the most widespread and open in the history of the modern games.

A New York Times inquiry into the drug situation at Munich disclosed that athletes from the Soviet Union, East Germany and several other Eastern European nations had access to large quantities of a new drug that could be taken as late as 15 minutes before competition to stimulate performances.

Extensive tests with 75 grams of the drug by Dr. David James, a 37-year-old chemist in Switzerland and former world-class sprinter from the United States, disclosed that its two major components were caffeine and nicotinamide, coupled with vitamins in the C and B complexes.

Neither ingredient was included on the list of banned drugs issued by the medical commission of the International Olympic Committee, although caffeine was on the original list drawn up by the commission six years ago.

COFFEE, NOT CIGARETTES

Caffeine is an alkaloid used in medicine as a cerebral and cardiac stimulant. It is most commonly associated as an ingredient in coffee (there are between 100 and 156 milligrams of caffeine in the average cup of coffee).

Nicotinamide is the amide of nicotinic acid, a vitamin and mild vasodilator that causes the blood vessels to enlarge, thereby increasing the flow of blood and theoretically increasing the oxygen supply to muscles. It is not to be confused with nicotine.

Asked what effects the drug had on the 30 Swiss athletes he tested after the Olympics, James said in a telephone interview from Lausanne:

"The persons' actions were more rapid, it seemed to delay fatigue, their reaction time was diminished, their motor activity was better."

The study by James follows disclosure of a formal protest to the I.O.C. by the United States Olympic Committee of 14 athletes, some of them medal winners, who reportedly took tranquilizers on the day of the shooting competition in the modern pentathlon.

TRANQUILIZERS NOT ON LIST

International pentathlon rules prohibit the use of tranquilizers, but the I.O.C. did not include tranquilizers on its list of forbidden drugs. In the Olympics. athletes compete under both I.O.C. and federation regulations.

"Through some sort of manipulation not clear to us," Clifford H. Buck, president of the U.S.O.C., said earlier this week in the pentathlon dispute, "the charges against the athletes were dropped and nothing was done about it."

Similar abuses occurred in the equestrian competition, according to Dr. Joseph O'Day, head veterinarian of the United States team. Dr. O'Day, a longtime Olympic observer, said that a recommendation for testing was made last May at a meeting of the International Equestrian Federation (F.E.I.), but was not implemented in Munich.

"I think there was evidence to me that tranquilizers were used in some horses, both in the three-day and crosscountry phase of the competition," said O'Day, who was instrumental in the establishment of testing procedures at horse shows in the United States.

O'Day confirmed that one horse died in Munich following post-race medication.

Thousands of athletes and medalwinners were subjected to what the I.O.C. terms doping control, but only 23 tests proved positive. One involved Rick DeMont, the 16-year-old American swimmer, who was stripped of his title in the 400-meter free-style and disqualified from the final of another race because his urinalysis turned up traces of ephedrine, a banned drug DeMont took as part of a medical prescription to curb asthma.

DeMont's disqualification disturbed many teammates, particularly when reports filtered out from the Olympic Village that some athletes were skirting doping procedures by taking drugs not banned by the I.O.C.

At least two American athletes — George Frenn, the hammer thrower, and Mrs. Olga Connolly, a five-time Olympic discus thrower — said that a former Soviet track and field athlete had told them that the Russians had developed a drug capable of stimulating an individual before competition.

"He said they had something that would make the muscles very explosive for a short period of time," Frenn said recently by phone from North Hollywood, Calif. "He also said they weren't using the drug in Munich, but I found that hard to believe."

ATHLETES TOLD JAMES

James, who finished third in the 1961 National Amateur Athletic Union outdoor track and field championships at Randalls Island (behind Frank Budd and Paul Drayton) and was clocked at 9.3 seconds for 100 yards, had been a resident of Switzerland since 1960. He was attached to the medical staff of the Swiss Olympic team when, he said, Swiss athletes approached him about the new drug being used by "Eastern athletes."

"One of my Swiss athletes obtained the drug from a Russian weight lifter and a Czechoslovak weight lifter," James said. James added that one of the weight lifters had used the drug in Munich.

"He came to a limit in his event and couldn't do very well," James said. "You have three tries in weight lifting. The first two didn't go too well, and the third, after he took a little of the drug, went very well."

Soviet sports officials repeatedly denied any knowledge of a new drug. James conceded it was possible that athletes could have taken the drug without the knowledge of coaches and officials.

James said the drug was in the form of a powder that could be taken outright or mixed with a drink. He declined to disclose where the drug was manufactured, the amount of caffeine ("there's enough in it to stimulate") or other sports where it was used at the Olympics besides weight lifting ("there were others, but I'd rather not name them").

James acknowledged, however, that a tablespoonful could carry as much stimulant impact as amphetamines, and that I.O.C. medical officials could do little under current procedures.

"I am basically against any kind of doping to augment the performance of an athlete," said James, who exhausted his supply of the drug administering the tests. "And it's very difficult to ban drug like caffeine. In shooting events [pistol] at the Olympics, they forbid all shooters to drink alcohol ... They could do the same thing for other people, if they wanted to, on the day they were competing, for caffeine."

Dr. Daniel F. Hanley, chairman of the U.S.O.C. medical and training services committee and a member of the medical commission in Munich, has done studies with caffeine. He issued a report on his findings earlier this year and noted that "caffeine did not improve performance and may even have been deleterious."

Hanley acknowledged, however, that caffeine had become a controversial drug in athletics because "the problem with banning it is that every country drinks coffee." Hanley said caffeine levels of athletes were picked up on a gas chromatograph in Munich, but would not show up in banned areas, because caffeine was not banned.

"The combination of caffeine and nicotinamide may well give athletes quite a feeling," Hanley said. "But I'd like to see the facts and figures on James's survey."

James attended the University of California, Los Angeles; California Institute of Technology, University of Geneva and received his medical degree from the University of Lausanne. He acquired Swiss citizenship last year and currently works at the Cantonal State Hospital in Lausanne.

Dr. Hans Howald, chief physician of the Swiss team, said James was well known in sports circles in Switzerland, particularly among track and field athletes, and "was accepted very well." Howald also described James as "very interested in sports medicine."

James said he was surprised at his findings, which raise a question on the effectiveness of doping control procedures.

"I felt there might be more of placebo effect," he said. "After seeing the ingredients, I think it is not so much of a placebo effect. I think it is more of a pharmacological effect. Together, they are a very powerful stimulant ... and they are drugs that should be banned for athletic uses."

For Olympic Hopefuls, Antidoping Rules Will Be an Adjustment

BY KAREN CROUSE | JAN. 25, 2015

AFTER CLOSING WITH a 62 at the Tournament of Champions this month, Chris Kirk showed up at the site of his next start and learned he had been randomly selected for out-of-competition testing as part of the PGA Tour's antidoping program.

The timing prompted Kirk, tongue in cheek, to post on Twitter: "Like clockwork, tie course record on Monday, drug test on Wednesday."

On Saturday, after his round at the Humana Challenge in La Quinta, Calif., Kirk said he was happy with "any and all drug testing." All golfers with gold medal aspirations should feel that way, because the antidoping program they are set to join is considerably less predictable and more invasive.

In advance of golf's return to the Olympics next year in Rio de Janeiro, the golfers will be under the aegis of the World Anti-Doping Agency. The agency operates its testing program much differently from what golfers, especially those from the United States, have come to expect. Consider Kirk, whose first exposure to drug testing, he said, was during his freshman year at Georgia. Describing the N.C.A.A. protocol, he said, "They'd notify you the afternoon before, and you had to be there the next morning at 6 a.m. to give a sample."

Kirk graduated to the program on the PGA Tour, in which players are targeted at tour sites. If they give urine samples on the Monday, Tuesday or Wednesday of a normal tournament week, that is considered out-of-competition testing.

Once under the Olympic umbrella, the golfers will be subject to unannounced testing at any time, including their off weeks. Brandt Snedeker, who has been critical of the tour's antidoping program, said: "The tour used to say they'd do that. It never really came to fruition."

Speaking after his Saturday round at the Humana Challenge,

Snedeker added, "I think it's something that every golfer is going to be a little shocked when it actually does happen."

As part of the Olympic antidoping program, golfers will have to provide the antidoping agency with a daily one-hour window of availability, listing when and where drug testers can find them, no matter where in the world they happen to be. In addition to urine, blood samples can also be collected.

"It's going to be different," Graeme McDowell said, "having the drug police knocking on your door at 5:30 in the morning."

McDowell, who is poised to represent Ireland at next year's Olympics, was speaking from last week's PGA Merchandise Show in Orlando, Fla. He appeared Wednesday on an Olympics forum alongside Suzann Pettersen, a top performer on the L.P.G.A. Tour; Gil Hanse and Amy Alcott, the architects of the 2016 Olympic course; and Peter Dawson, the International Golf Federation president.

Pettersen, 33, who is from Norway, said she was unfazed by the prospect of more stringent drug testing. She said she had to submit to regular and random drug testing from her national federation when she was a teenager.

"The procedure that we're facing is nothing compared to my fellow Norwegian athletes," she said. "They have to report their whereabouts 24/7, and if you're not at the spot you said you were going to be, that's almost the same as failing a drug test."

From her perspective, the more stringent testing for the world's golfers cannot start soon enough. "I know some of the Swedish athletes have joked and said, 'Why don't you install a GPS in us, and you'll know where we are all the time?' " she said. "The pressure of always being on top of your schedule can be a pain, but for me, clean sport has always been a top priority."

When will the golfers become subject to the antidoping agency's testing policies? McDowell said it was his understanding that it would be during the 13-week period leading up to the Olympics, which are scheduled to start Aug. 5 of next year. He was echoing the time frame set forth by Dawson, who said the golfers would be under the agency's umbrella starting three months before the Olympics. "I think that's it," he said.

According to an official with the United States Anti-Doping Agency, pro athletes historically enter the registered testing pool 12 months before the Olympics, and the plans being completed for golf follow that timetable.

The prevailing view in golf is that drug testing is unnecessary because it is a clean sport whose practitioners consider cheating abhorrent. Speaking for that majority, Snedeker said: "I want the playing field level. I just think in the other sports, there's so much to be gained by doing P.E.D.s," or performance-enhancing drugs.

He added: "I get it when you're talking about a hundredth of a second being the difference between winning an Olympic medal and not winning an Olympic medal. But with golf, I still remain skeptical."

Ask most golfers why athletes take performance-enhancing drugs, and they will say it is to add muscle. But the drugs can also be used to help athletes recover faster from heavy training or injuries, as the players were reminded recently when one of their own on the Web.com Tour, the Class AAA of golf, received a one-year suspension for violating the PGA Tour's antidoping policy. That golfer, Bhavik Patel, a native Californian who played for Fresno State, did not appeal his punishment. "In an effort to overcome an injury, I made a lapse of judgment," he said.

McDowell said it was important for those in golf to take the Olympic antidoping program seriously. "It's going to be very insightful for us as a sport, as a game, as professional athletes, to experience what those other sports have to put up with," he said. "I'm not going to say we'll embrace it. We will accept it."

He added: "Part of the whole growing process to become an Olympic sport was to step up to the plate and really be responsible professional athletes and toe the line. We shouldn't have anything to hide, and that's the bottom line."

CHAPTER 2

Limits of Protection

The establishment of antidoping tests and protocols came with controversies and objections. Because antidoping protocols were created at different times and with different standards depending on the sport, inconsistencies were bound to happen. Problems encountered with setting up antidoping procedures took the efforts of a number of dedicated professionals to fix. The advancement of medical science also affected testing standards and efforts as some of the drugs previously outlawed were reconsidered.

Strike Keeps Tour de France Riders on Pills and Needles

BY JOHN L. HESS | JULY 10, 1966

TURIN, ITALY, JULY 9 — With the bicycle riders in the Tour de France resting here today before heading for home through the Great Saint Bernard Pass tomorrow, nobody is saying the nasty word "doping" any more.

The affair began in Bordeaux following the eighth day of the 22-day grind when gendarmes and physicians in the pay of the Sports Ministry burst into boudoirs for a random sampling of bikers.

NEEDLED RIDERS COMPLAIN

The physicians demanded and obtained urine specimens from a score of athletes while the lawmen went through their baggage. French policemen can be charming in giving directions to the ladies, but they are sometimes impulsive in other duties.

The following day in the foothills of the Pyrenees, the racing pack suddenly dismounted and silently walked 100 yards or so pushing the bicycles. Having made their point, they remounted and headed for the hills.

Nobody denied that the riders were getting synthetic help. "But why pick on us?" they demanded. Why not, they asked, go after the student taking benzedrine before an exam or the businessman gulping tranquilizers? Why not go after amateur athletes? ...

The immediate answer was that enforcement had to begin somewhere, that the cyclists' use of the needle was notorious and that the Tour de France was a conspicuous place for the authorities to tell the sports world they meant business.

But the stoppage seems to have worked. There have been no more inspections and the results of the Bordeaux analyses have not been announced. The guess among the cynical sports writers here is that they never will be.

TESSEYRE JEAN/PARIS MATCH ARCHIVE/GETTY IMAGES

Riders at the 1966 Tour de France work their way uphill during a mountain stage of the competition.

The feeling is that an anti-drugging law may be unenforceable.

The big problem is how to define drugging. In justifying himself, a star racer touched on this point.

"When you get up in the morning," he asked, "do you need a cup of coffee to get started? Well, after doing 150 miles the day before, we might need three or four coffees."

In the race, riders carry flasks of coffee, cubes of sugar and other fortifying things. Nobody questions their right to all the carbohydrates, proteins, minerals and vitamins they need.

When they are in pain, which is often, nobody can question their right to sedation. But some painkillers, tranquilizers, caffeine and vitamins in certain doses can spur a man or a horse to go faster than he normally would. The trainers, with or without medical degrees, all are supposed to have their personal recipes.

"My man knows what's good for me," the star said.

There is the rub, in the view of the authorities. The doses administered in tough competition may be good for the performance; they are not good for the performers.

It is widely believed that many bad spills are caused by over drugged riders. And nobody could call the wan, skinny heroes of this race a picture of health.

But how can society protect the athletes against themselves? Judging from the Tour de France, the answer has not been found.

Outcry on Wider Use of Drugs for Race Horses

BY STEVE CADY | MARCH 29, 1977

IT HAPPENS EVERY DAY at tracks in all but six of the 25 states where pari-mutuel racing takes place: Horses with sore legs or other ailments, the kind of problems that formerly could be cured only by rest, parade to the post under the influence of once-forbidden drugs.

Until five or six years ago, use of the drugs after a horse had been entered for a race was prohibited by most states. But the economic and legislative pressures of year-round racing, with its emphasis on tax revenue, has produced a more permissive attitude. Nineteen states now allow horses to race with once-banned drugs such as Butazolidin (an analgesic) and Lasix (a diuretic) in their systems. Of the major racing states, only New York maintains a ban on medication of any kind, even an aspirin, for racing purposes. Liberal drug rules exist now in such major horse areas as California, Florida, Kentucky, Maryland and Illinois.

Growing evidence of abuses has touched off a fresh controversy over permissive medication. Is it a boon for racing, as most horse trainers contend? Or is it a boondoggle that permits trainers and veterinarians to manipulate the form of horses and thus defraud the public? Is it humane or inhumane?

Recent developments have raised serious questions about the wisdom of a laissez-faire drug policy. In Pennsylvania, where four times as many breakdowns have occurred since the 1975 legalization of Butazolidin, the Society for the Prevention of Cruelty to Animals has begun a campaign to have the drug banned outright. In New York, an interim report by the State Racing and Wagering Board found Butazolidin and Lasix to be "just the tip of the iceberg" in the drug problem.

Caught in the middle of the controversy are the state racing commissions that regulate the industry. As political appointees, the commissioners don't have to be reminded about the importance of tax revenue. On the other hand, they have a responsibility to protect the racing public and even the horses that put on the show.

THE BACKGROUND

In 1948, the year Citation won the Triple Crown, thoroughbred racing had no trouble keeping its parimutuel wheel of fortune spinning smoothly with only about 5,000 new foals a year. Northern racing seasons opened in April and closed in November, leaving plenty of time for horses to be rested.

If the word "drug" was used in horse racing, the reference almost always involved a case in which a horse had been "hopped up" with a stimulant. But racing's popularity, combined with government's search for tax revenue, gradually led to a saturation of the market. Racing seasons everywhere were extended, additional states legalized parimutuel gambling, new tracks were built and the number of racing dates increased greatly.

To meet the demand for horseflesh, breeders stepped up their production, often with little regard for the quality or soundness of the offspring. About 28,000 thoroughbred foals are born each year now on American farms, but even that supply is barely enough to satisfy the needs of year-round racing at so many tracks. As track complaints about the shortage of able-bodied horses grew, the campaign for permissive medication intensified.

Yet the shadowy subject of equine medication didn't come to public attention until 1968, when Dancer's Image won the Kentucky Derby and then was ordered disqualified because a postrace urinalysis allegedly showed he had run with Butazolidin in his system. Headlines in several newspapers read: "Derby Winner Doped." But Butazolidin, or "bute," as horsemen call it, is not dope in the sense that a stimulant or a depressant is dope. It won't make a horse run faster or slower than its normal speed. Nor is it a true painkiller, like Novocain.

Butazolidin, the trade name for phenylbutazone, is an analgestic that eases pain by reducing inflammation in muscles or joints. It supposedly enables a horse to perform to the best of its ability. That Dancer's Image had a suspicious ankle the week of the Derby lent weight to the medication ruling, but the verdict was appealed in a bizarre case that dragged on through several years of hearings and courtroom battles.

Eventually, the Kentucky Court of Appeals overruled a lower-court decision that the state chemist had not proved the presence of bute. Today, the medication is as much a part of racing as boots and saddles. So is Lasix, a medication used ostensibly to control the respiratory ailment that causes certain horses to bleed through the nostrils.

FOR MEDICATION

Those who favor the policy stress that human athletes have competed for decades with the aid of anti-inflammatory agents like Butazolidin. Some vets see bute as nothing more sinister than a "super aspirin" that eases various types of arthritic aches and pains. Other vets have questioned the assumption that the drug enables a lame horse to run without sensing pain.

"Butazolidin helps the body chemically to heal itself," says Dr. Leonard Foote, secretary of the California Horse Racing Board. "The pain goes away quickly only because the horse heals faster with the help of bute."

Another state vet in California, Dr. Lindley Allen, says the medication program there has worked well. Among the benefits, he feels, are a reduction of drug experimentation, reduced use of steroids, decrease in race-day scratches and a stronger role for vets (rather than trainers) in the treatment of horses.

Dr. Joseph O'Dea, vet for the United States Equestrian Team's horses at last year's Olympics, has been one of the most vocal supporters of Butazolidin. He calls it, a "helpful medication" that should not be blamed for any increase in breakdowns.

Tracks now post medication lists for each day's racing and publish the information in The Daily Racing Form. In states such as

California, postrace chemical tests include a "no bute" finding, under which a trainer can be penalized if the test fails to show bute in the system of a horse that has supposedly been running on it.

Perhaps the key question is whether most tracks, particularly smaller ones that rely on cheaper horses, can continue to function without permissive medication.

AGAINST MEDICATION

Opponents of permissive medication, a group that appears to be gaining support, tend to blame the problem on the greed or indifference of state legislators, trainers, drug salesmen and profit-minded tracks. The critics argue that horses whose pain has been eased by medications (injected or ground up in feed) are more apt to break down because of the stress the animals put on unsound legs that otherwise would flash danger signals.

Another major indictment against the unregulated use of Butazolidin and Lasix is that they can mask other drugs, such as stimulants and tranquilizers, that are still prohibited in all states. The University of Kentucky, for example, found that Lasix can make the presence of powerful drugs like Methadone virtually undetectable. Bute, it is said, can mask at least a dozen other acidbased drugs.

Lasix has proved to be an effective drug for so-called bleeders. But only about 2 percent of the 50,000 thoroughbreds that raced in North America last year were known bleeders, while as many as three of every four horses racing at tracks with an unrestricted Lasix policy used the drug. In 1975 Florida reported that 72 percent of the horses racing there were on bute, 75 percent on Lasix.

New York's Racing and Wagering Board, in the interim report it issued last August, found the sudden and dramatic increase of bleeders a "highly suspicious" development.

"Lasix causes excessive urination," said Dr. James Manning, the state vet at Saratoga Raceway. "This tends to flush the other drugs out of a horse's system, or at least lower their levels so they can't be detected. I think the medication rule in New York should be left the way it is. It would be great if you could allow horses with only minor ailments to race on medication, but it wouldn't work. The trainers would treat everything, and people would be trying to get a 'last race' out of horses that shouldn't be racing.

Horses at New York tracks, thoroughbred or standardbred, can be trained on medication, even though they can't run on it. The same rule applies in New Jersey, with the single exception that horses certified by the state vet to be known bleeders can be given Lasix before a race.

THE OUTLOOK

At the time of the Dancer's Image case in 1968, only two states (Colorado and Nebraska) allowed horses to race with bute in their systems. In 1971 California became the third state to permit it.

Despite the current widespread use of permissive medication, several states are beginning to have second thoughts. Crash programs in equine drug research have started at a number of facilities. And there is a growing suspicion that state racing chemists have not been keeping pace with the development of new drugs.

New York's racing board said in its interim report, "Pharmaceutical houses spend millions of dollars each year creating not only the drugs themselves, but a market for their use."

The latest example of uncertainty over the effectiveness of drug-track testing facilities occurred a week ago when the New York State Testing Laboratory in Jamaica, Queens, was quietly phased out. During 1973 it reported no "positives" in 17,056 official urine and saliva samples from racing at New York's four thoroughbred tracks. It was closed because of what the board called its "inability to function in an acceptable manner."

All chemical testing for New York tracks is now conducted by the State College of Veterinary Medicine at Cornell University, a facility that has consistently spotted more drug violations since it began testing samples (by blood and urinalysis) a few years ago.

New York horsemen have demanded "immediate action" by the racing board to institute a permissive-medication rule. But Joseph H. Boyd Jr., the board member in charge of the committee studying the problem, is in no hurry to jump to conclusions.

"The new 48-hour rule on entering horses should help a lot," Boyd said. "It's a new ball game with that rule, because medications should be out of the system within 48 hours. But the biggest problem in this whole issue is that we haven't done enough research. That's what we need."

Effect of Drugs to Aid Athletes Studied by U.S.

BY THE NEW YORK TIMES | AUG. 22, 1976

MINUTES AFTER HIS second-place finish in the Olympic Marathon at Montreal, Frank Shorter was asked whether he might be tempted to try for a gold medal at the 1980 Olympics in Moscow.

"Yeah," Shorter said somewhat cynically, "if I find some good doctors."

Shorter's words may be answered. The United States Olympic Committee has quietly approved the formation of a panel of experts to study the scientific and medical aspects of sports and their effect on the performances of world-class athletes.

The success or failure of the panel could determine America's future role in international sports competition.

DARDIK IN CHARGE

Coordinating the program will be Dr. Irving Dardik, an aggressive 40-year-old cardiovascular surgeon from Tenafly, N. J., who was a member of the U.S.O.C. medical staff in Montreal and is understood to have the respect and confidence of many American athletes.

Dardik said the panel would be formed immediately and would explore a variety of areas — nutritional, pharmacological and advanced medical approaches to training. Prominent physicians, orthopedic surgeons, exercise physiologists and pharmacologists in the United States would be contacted about contributing knowledge and research to the program.

"We want to develop methods and modalities for working with athletes that would enhance their performances and be safe," Dardik said, during a recent interview. "We'll be reviewing as much information as we can in the European sector, directly and indirectly, and explore what's been done elsewhere.

"We'll be working predominantly from the medical side and dealing with the top athletes in all sports."

Dardik said the panel was prepared to "look into areas considered taboo" in sports and make judgements on the benefit or harm to American athletes. This would include extensive research into the effects of anabolic steroids and blood-doping on performance.

United States athletes have long contended that Eastern European countries had developed sophisticated sports medicine programs that contributed significantly to the performances of their athletes and placed Americans at a disadvantage. The gold-medal output of East Germany and the Soviet Union in Montreal only reaffirmed this belief in the minds of many American competitors.

CHANGED RELATIONS

Although the study of sports medicine has increased in the United States in recent years, the U.S.O.C. had considered its relationship with athletes more advisory than personal. With the blessing of Col. Don Miller, the U.S.O.C. executive director, Dardik said the panel was prepared to assist any athlete.

"I don't buy the concept that we shouldn't have to go that far to achieve success," Dardik said. "That's too much like sour grapes. All we're going to do now is tell the athletes everything they want to know or need to know and let them make a judgement on what they feel is important to them."

Dardik said medicine is likely to assume an even greater role in future international sports competition, an opinion that is shared by Dr. John Anderson, another member of the U.S.O.C. medical staff.

IMPACT OF MEDICINE

"It's become a medical Olympics," Anderson said, referring to the elaborate testing procedures adopted under doping control. "Twenty-five percent of our time in Montreal was spent on trying to explain to athletes all the details of the tests and the drugs that they could and couldn't take. It's gone too far."

Anderson cited the case of Mac Wilkins, the Olympic discus champion, as an example of the inconsistencies in doping control. Wilkins was tested twice for steroids — the day he arrived at the Olympic Village and the day after his competition — but was never tested by the International Olympic Committee in their routine-post-event procedures.

"I don't blame Wilkins for being upset about this," Anderson said. "An athlete can become bewildered over why he's being called so often. It doesn't make too much sense."

The random steroid tests in Montreal were conducted by the various sports federations. Anderson conceded that the emphasis was geared to weight-type events.

Dardik believes the panel will provide a resource unit for athletes. At the United States Olympic track and field trials, in Eugene, Ore., 23 athletes failed the doping control test.

Most of the positive results were attributed to pills for hay fever and allergy-related symptoms brought on by a high pollen count. Dardik stressed the need for a consistent policy in the future at all national championships and American trials.

"We've got to prepare our athletes the same way they would be treated at an Olympics," Dardik said.

Dardik realizes that the panel will be on the spot in view of the publicity over drugs and the private theories surrounding the gold-medal performances of some European athletes in Montreal.

"This is not — I repeat — not going to be a committee that is being formed to take the heat off," he said. "I'm prepared to do whatever the athletes want to help them for Moscow. But we want to do it so that the athletes understand each step along the way."

Dardik said steroids would be a major source of inquiry, particularly those elements such as androgens that deal with muscle building. Tests with animals could be used, along with specifically controlled programs for athletes, at their wishes.

Steroids are chemical compounds that have been declared illegal, for Olympic competition. Three major classifications have become popularized under the adrenal series — cortisone, aldosterone and endrogens. Naturally occurring chemicals such as testosterone reportedly also have been developed that skirt Olympic testing procedures.

A number of athletes, including one American weightlifter, Mark Cameron, were disqualified in Montreal because of positive steroid test results. In 1972, an asthmatic United States swimmer, Rick DeMont, was forced to return a gold medal because tracing of the drug ephedrine showed up in his urinanalysis.

Another source of medical and ethical debate in Montreal was blood doping. Under this program developed in several Scandinavian countries, an athlete gives up a pint of blood at a prescribed time, the blood is preserved while the athlete continues high-level training and then is injected back into his system at a prescribed period before his competition.

Lasse Viren of Finland, who won the 10,000 and 5,000-meter gold medals for a second consecutive time in Montreal, became the focus of most of the blood-doping rumors. However, Viren denied knowledge of the procedure although it remains legal.

"I want the athletes to talk to us," Dirdik said. "If a marathon runner like Frank Shorter believes blood-doping be a major source of inquiry, was the reason he lost in the Olympics, I want him to tell us. Then we can start researching this and tell Frank what we've found."

Can such an ambitious undertaking become functional enough to have any impact for Moscow?

"If anyone can make it happen, Irv Dardik can," said Willye White, five-time United States Olympic long jumper. "This is the kind of program we've needed for a long time. If the U.S.O.C. lets Dardik operate, there's no telling how far we could go."

After a three-hour session with Miller, and discussion with other U.S.O.C. medical officials, Dardik is convinced the program can work.

"I wouldn't take it up if I didn't believe in it," he said. "I don't like to lose; I don't think our athletes like it; and I know the American public has the best interest of our athletes at heart."

Study May Renew 'Blood Doping' Debate

BY NEIL AMDUR | MAY 4, 1980

TOM WALSH FELT it gave him the racer's edge. Tim Ward said "it was a great feeling, unbelievable, I knew I wasn't going to die." Larry Shofe did not even feel like he had run five miles.

Those reactions, from three members of the Tidewater (Va.) Striders, followed their experience with a controlled experiment in "blood doping," the controversial technique of withdrawing some of an athlete's blood and returning it to the body at a later date to aid athletic performance.

Twelve long-distance runners affiliated with the Striders, 11 of whom had run marathons, participated in the eight-month study at the Human Performance Laboratory of Old Dominion University in Norfolk, Va. According to Dr. Melvin H. Williams, who coordinated the project and also participated in it, the results proved conclusively that blood doping can increase the performance capacity of athletes in endurance events.

Dr. Williams's study, which he reported on last weekend at a meeting of the Rocky Mountain chapter of the American College of Sports Medicine, is certain to intensify efforts for a more thorough review of the issue. It may also prompt revisions in training techniques for sports such as running, rowing, swimming, soccer and cross-country skiing.

SOME OF THE FINDINGS

"As a coach, I deal a lot with psychology," said Shofe, the 26-year-old swimming coach at Old Dominion, whose time on a laboratory treadmill improved by 2 minutes 12 seconds after blood doping. "We shave down for big meets and use other training aids. If I could, I'd like to try the blood reinfusion on distance swimmers. Physiologically and psychologically, knowing what I know now after these tests, there have to be great benefits."

Some of the more significant findings from the Old Dominion study were as follows:

- Eleven of the 12 runners improved their five-mile times on a treadmill from earlier tests after having received their blood back. The average time of improvement for the group was an astonishing 44 seconds, or almost nine seconds a mile.

- The hemoglobin levels of the runners, an important consideration in evaluating endurance capability, increased substantially during the post blood period, from an average of 15.0 to 16.1.

- The ratings of perceived exertion — a symbol of how runners felt on the treadmill — were significantly lower during the first two miles of the post-blood tests compared with the other three tests.

- The average time for the final mile in the post-blood test was 17 seconds faster than any average mile during the other tests and 11 seconds faster (a 5:44 average) than the first four miles (a 5:55 average) in the post-blood test.

"I definitely felt better in the homestretch," said Walsh, a 37-year-old counselor at a juvenile and domestic court in Virginia Beach. "It was like a shot in the arm."

NUMEROUS STUDIES

As many as 16 studies into blood doping have been done in Europe, Canada and the United States — with varying results — since a Swedish researcher, Bjorn Ekblom, concluded in the early 1970's that increased blood volume contributes to increased oxygen capacity and in turn performance levels. The controversy has been fueled by reports that the practice helped Lasse Viren of Finland win successive Olympic gold medals at 5,000 and 10,000 meters in Munich and Montreal.

Viren, who is scheduled to compete today against top Americans in the 15-kilometer Midland Run in Far Hills, N.J., has repeatedly denied the charge. The International Olympic Committee does not monitor blood doping.

Dr. Williams conducted two earlier studies on blood doping, as well as extensive research into the possible effects of caffeine, hypnosis and amphetamines on athletic performance. "This is the first one in which we found any significant improvement," he said during a phone interview last Friday from Norfolk.

Dr. Williams received a grant of $1,100 from the Old Dominion School of Education Research Fund for his study.

He attributed the statistical improvement to a larger amount of blood and the simulation of racing conditions.

In earlier experiments, the metric equivalent of one pint of blood was used. For this study, which began in May 1979 and concluded last February, 920 milliliters, or almost two pints of blood, were taken from the runners — first one pint, then another eight weeks later — before two "learning trials" and the testing began.

The runners were tested four times after the blood was removed, in groups of six, using a saline solution as a control for one series of tests, blood for the other, and then reversing the procedure. The post-blood treadmill test in the double-blind project was usually administered one or two days after the runners had received the blood.

Most of the runners, including Dr. Williams, said they were not aware whether they had received blood or the saline solution, but they soon sensed a difference in their performance that they attributed to reinfusion.

"When I was running, I never felt that way before," said Shofe, who runs distances primarily from 10,000 meters to 10 miles. "I noticed something after the first mile. My wind wasn't bothering me, and I kept asking them to turn up the speed. At the end, I didn't think I had run the race. I think I could have gone another five miles."

Ward, the physical education director of the Norfolk Y.M.C.A., said he saw nothing illegal in the practice. "To me," the 28-year-old Ward said, "it's like taking a vitamin. It's one more edge. When you're talking about a world-class athlete, it could be crucial."

There were noticeable side effects to the early loss of the blood, which was frozen by Red Cross workers assisting in the experiment. Some runners complained of weariness and training fatigue. "When they took it out initially, I was wiped out," Ward said. Others found themselves urinating more frequently after reinfusion.

None of the 12 runners were at the world-class level. The fastest five-mile treadmill time among the group was 26:22, although a number had broken three hours in a marathon.

"We don't know how blood doping would affect world-class runners," Williams said. "They may be at a level where they already are reaching their maximum performance capacity. Then again, maybe they aren't. I'd like to set up a laboratory study in the field. It would be like looking at it during an actual run. Hopefully, we can plan something like this for next year."

I.O.C. Issues Doping Report

BY THE NEW YORK TIMES | AUG. 4, 1980

MOSCOW, AUG. 3 — The medical commission of the International Olympic Committee reported today that no athletes had been caught using proscribed drugs at the Moscow Olympics, but said that did not mean they had not been doing so.

Prince Alexandre de Merode, chairman of the commission, said at a news conference today that the main reason for doubt was that there is no reliable test to determine whether athletes take the male hormone testosterone externally.

"You see some of the shapes," Prof. Arnold H. Beckett, a member of the commission, said, "and suspicions are probably justified." Some East German women swimmers emerged from the waves with what appeared to be un-Botticelli curves and deep voices, a phenomenon that has attracted notice not only at these Games.

The problem, Dr. Beckett said, is that athletes who use the banned anabolic steroid drugs to build up body weight and increase performance can discontinue its use in time before a competition, to avoid detection. By taking testosterone afterward, they can also avoid any drop in performance.

Varying Standards on Steroid Use

BY WILLIAM C. RHODEN | OCT. 2, 1988

THE DESIRE TO ENHANCE athletic performance is one of man's oldest pursuits, traceable, perhaps, to that point in time when speed, strength and agility became recreational pursuits rather than survival techniques.

In the last two decades, as speed and strength have opened the door to financial opportunities as well, a perplexing marriage between sports and drugs has been forged.

Over the years, the reason for drug use in athletics has remained the same: the pursuit of a winning edge. But last week in Seoul, the quest for that edge may have pushed tolerance for performance-enhancing drugs to a breaking point.

The world was stunned when the Canadian runner Ben Johnson, who had won the 100-meter dash in record time three days earlier,

BOB THOMAS/BOB THOMAS SPORTS PHOTOGRAPHY/GETTY IMAGES

Ben Johnson finished first in the 100 meters at the 1988 Olympics but was disqualified three days later after failing a drug test.

tested positive for stanozolol, an anabolic steroid. Within hours, Mr. Johnson was stripped of his record and his medal, banned from international competition for two years and prohibited for life from competing with a Canadian national team.

The next day, Juan Antonio Samaranch, the International Olympic Committee president, said of the event: "It will demonstrate to the world where we stand on doping."

Unexpectedly, Mr. Johnson's banishment has shed light on what has been a considerably more casual attitude toward steroids by professional-sports groups in this country.

As he was being penalized before an international audience, 75 reporters waited at Giants Stadium for the return of Lawrence Taylor, the all-Pro linebacker for the New York Giants.

TALE OF TWO ATHLETES

Mr. Taylor was suspended on Aug. 29 when he tested positive for cocaine use. It was his second offense. That meant an automatic suspension and mandatory drug rehabilitation.

For the most part, Mr. Johnson's banishment and Mr. Taylor's return were unrelated dramas. Yet they illustrate the disparity in perspective between amateur and professional-sports groups, particularly the National Football League, regarding steroids. The incidents also illustrate the N.F.L.'s approach to the years-old problem of steroids.

Just hours after Mr. Johnson's censure, the professionals came calling. Three football teams, two of them from the N.F.L., made overtures to Mr. Johnson's agent.

Had Mr. Taylor tested positive for steroids instead of cocaine, he would not have faced a single penalty.

"There is a distinction being made between steroids and pot and cocaine," said Joe Browne, the director of communications for the N.F.L.

One reason for the distinction, Mr. Browne said, is that cocaine and marijuana are illegal. "The other reason," he said, "is that the methodology for the testing is still evolving. We want to take a hard look after this season to see what the latest information on steroid use in the league is."

Certain drugs can mask the use of steroids within five to seven days of an event, and are virtually undetectable.

Many adverse side effects, including reproductive abnormalities and liver diseases, have been attributed to steroid use.

SECOND CHANCE

The N.F.L. began testing for steroids last year. Unlike the amateur organizations, however, the league has taken a kid-gloves approach to players identified as steroid users. If a player tests positive twice, he is subject to discipline by the commissioner. There have been no suspensions so far.

"To my knowledge, we're not actively testing people for steroids with the idea of doing anything in a treatment sense," said Dr. Charles Brown, the past president of the N.F.L. Physicians Society.

A year ago, he said, several N.F.L. linemen received letters telling them that that they had tested positive for steroids. Dr. Brown said most of them justified using steroids by saying that opponents also did.

A poignant statement on the situation was made last winter by Dave Cadigan, the New York Jets rookie offensive tackle: "I played against a lot of guys that I know for a fact were using steroids. I played them one year, the next year they come back 15 pounds heavier, stronger and they looked different. They played better and hit harder. That was one piece of the pie in my decision. I will do anything to become the best lineman in the N.F.L."

Dr. Charles Yeslis, professor of health policy and administration at Penn State University, says that because of a lack of data, he feels the scare has been exaggerated following the events in Seoul but that "there are reasons to be concerned about steroids."

"One," he said, "they work. Two, we don't know the long-term health effect. The third issue is the issue of fair play. Clearly, steroids give you an advantage over people who aren't taking them."

For the N.F.L.'s physicians, fair play is a central issue. When some players take steroids and others don't, Dr. Brown said, "competition at that level is no longer equal."

There are indications that the N.F.L. will soon take a stronger stand against steroid users. In June, the league's physicians urged the N.F.L. to adopt a strong policy toward steroids. And one general manager said last week, "It's going to be dealt with and dealt with harshly."

Gary Wadler, Antidoping Pioneer, Had a Gift for Straight Talk

BY JULIET MACUR | SEPT. 13, 2017

WHILE ON A TRIP to Stockholm nearly a decade ago, Gary Wadler and his wife, Nancy, visited the palace, where they were offered a chance to pose for a photograph with Queen Silvia of Sweden. Just before the camera clicked, Wadler threw his arm around the queen and flashed a big smile, just as he might have posed with an old friend.

The room fell silent. Soon the Wadlers could hear murmurs.

" 'Oh, my God, he's touching the queen! He's touching the queen!' " Nancy Wadler recalled people whispering. "Whoops, I guess you weren't supposed to touch the queen."

But that snapshot was consummate Wadler, the antidoping pioneer who died Tuesday at age 78. The son of a Brooklyn window-trimmer, Wadler was friendly, not formal. Studied, but never staid.

He grew up to be a doctor and a professor of medicine at New York University, and approachability was always one of his biggest assets. It's part of the reason he served for decades as an unofficial translator of the subject of performance-enhancing drugs.

When reporters called Wadler for his guidance while covering one drug scandal or another — and I can't count the number of times I called — he didn't overwhelm them with scientific or medical jargon. In the same manner in which he might deal with a patient in his internist's practice on Long Island, Wadler was always patient, always helpful, always eager to dumb down highly technical terms without making the questioner feel dumb.

Wadler didn't mind the tutorials. In fact, he thought they were vital. He often talked to me about how important it was that the public understand that steroids and other performance-enhancing drugs could be dangerous — to elite athletes, for sure, but to young ones, too. Wadler feared ignorance more than the drugs themselves, just as he worried that "steroid fatigue" would keep people from caring.

Long before the Bay Area Laboratory Co-operative steroids scandal, and way before Lance Armstrong came clean, Wadler was telling Americans that doping in sports was a scourge. Wadler knew so much about antidoping science and the culture of doping in sports that he wrote a seminal book, "Drugs and the Athlete," which was published in 1989, years before the subject of steroids became a standard feature of the sports pages.

"I grew up believing that our sports heroes were genuine, that they were great athletes because they had special skills and trained harder," he told Newsday in 2003.

But he also understood how much times had changed.

When Taylor Hooton, a teenage Texas pitcher, committed suicide in 2003 after stopping his steroid use, Hooton's father, Don, reached out to Wadler for answers to his many questions.

"Over many calls and many hours, he educated me and pointed me to reading material, helping me understand what anabolic steroids are and what they do to the mind and body," Don Hooton said Wednesday. "Some of these experts start off with going into all the technical stuff with doping, and they can lose you really quick. But Gary put things in a way that I could understand, and was so compassionate."

Wadler later encouraged Hooton to start a foundation to fight steroid use among young people, and went on to serve as its chairman.

But he also testified to Congress during the 2005 baseball steroid hearings. He criticized the WWE for not doing enough to combat drug use in professional wrestling, and he questioned the N.F.L.'s drug-testing program because he found it odd that more players were not testing positive in a sport in which athletes could surely benefit from banned drugs.

More times than I can count, Wadler called the N.F.L.'s rules "blatantly ridiculous" when we spoke about them.

"It took guts to stand up to so many people and so many leagues like he did," Nancy Wadler said. "But I like the truth. Gary liked the truth."

That truth went both ways. When the former N.F.L. lineman Lyle Alzado was dying of brain cancer in 1991, he blamed his many years of steroid and human growth hormone use. Some were happy to let this idea circulate widely, perhaps to scare younger athletes away from steroid use. But Wadler said, no, there wasn't actually a scientific connection between steroids and cancer. Wadler didn't ring alarm bells just to ring them.

It didn't take long for his reputation to spread internationally. He was a founding member of the World Anti-Doping Agency when it was formed in 2000, and at one point he led the committee that determined what substances would be on the agency's banned list.

"I didn't know much about him when he appeared at WADA, but I soon realized that this is a man who knows what he is talking about," said Arne Ljungqvist, a former chairman of the International Olympic Committee's medical commission, who met Wadler soon after WADA was formed.

Ljungqvist said WADA's prohibited-substance committee initially was filled with researchers like him and experts in subjects like pharmacology, hematology and chemistry, a group that he said was heavy on credentials and missing a common touch. Wadler, he found, provided a refreshing perspective.

"As a medical doctor, he filled a gap which made the commission complete," Ljungqvist said. "He had knowledge that some didn't. I looked upon him as one of my best friends."

Ljungqvist liked Wadler because he had a lot of common sense, and because he wasn't the type of man who would promote himself. Wadler was just so very likable, said Ljungqvist, who was the person who arranged Wadler's meeting with Queen Silvia.

A day after Wadler died, Nancy Wadler told me that Queen Silvia story. In a conversation that lasted most of the morning, she laughed a lot. And she cried some, too.

She said she had been going through their belongings lately, and among them she had found a gigantic teddy bear candle he had given her when they began dating in the early 1970s. They were married for 45 years, and often discussed why their relationship lasted that long.

"It's really a mirror of honesty, having principles you live by, integrity and giving back to the world," Nancy Wadler said. "You could say that also was his philosophy about his doping work."

CHAPTER 3

Bucking the System

Whenever there are rules, there are people who try to break them. When it comes to doping, those efforts have sometimes been sponsored by whole countries, as with Russia. The competition is fierce in professional sports and the Olympics, with the stakes including fame, money and national pride. While some athletes and organizations have offered little more than lip service against doping, others have objected to the punitive nature of antidoping tests. One thing is certain: doping will continue to be restricted as much as possible.

Turf Authorities Are Accused of 'Silence' Plot in Drugging

BY JOHN L. HESS | FEB. 20, 1966

PARIS, FEB. 19 — Dr. Robert S. Aries, whose activities in the patents field have kept scores of lawyers gainfully employed for years, has accused horse racing authorities of "a conspiracy of silence" about drugging techniques.

Aries, a former professor of chemistry at Brooklyn Polytechnic Institute, is the author and publisher of textbooks on drugging.

He also is the organizer and president of a society to study the techniques and detection of art forgery and has been accused in the United States, Switzerland and France of the theft of patents, which he, in turn, accused drug companies of stealing from him.

More recently he came into the public eye when he and two companies registered in Monaco some 335 trade names, many of them world known. He subsequently wrote a stern lecture to the business world on its negligence in protecting its valuable titles.

HOLDS DUAL CITIZENSHIP

Dr. Aries, who appears to have dual citizenship (in the United States and France), turned out also to be a member of a Trademark Protective Association here.

In art and horseracing, as in patents and trademarks, Dr. Aries makes plain that he is horrified at the laxity of the authorities, the weakness of detection techniques and the temptations thus presented to unscrupulous men.

He says racing authorities hamper honest researchers. By contrast anybody can obtain, for $11 postpaid, Aries's treatise, "The Doping of Race Horses: Study of the Medicaments Used." The book, 62 mimeographed pages in French, is Monaco, one of the companies that registered the trade names along with Dr. Aries.

The author stoutly maintains that doping horses is wrong. He says it's dangerous for animals, jockeys and bettors; threatens the improvement of the breed, and is bad for business, since if the public gets the notion that races are crooked, "adieu le clients."

But he warns that the technology of drugging has been galloping along, while that of detection has been left at the post. He lists scores of new biochemical products — vitamins, hormones, cortisone, tranquillizers, etc. — that can in improper dosages help a horse to win — or lose — a race. He also gives the improper dosages for horses, greyhounds and, most deplorably in his view, for human athletes.

As with trademarks, Aries finds the law on drugging full of loopholes. Citing an early definition of doping as anything given a horse to stimulate its performance, he comments that any rich feed produces stimulants in the animal. If this argument is "Jesuitical," he continues, what about vitamins, hormones and painkillers?

"What is more natural than to treat a horse that has a cold?" Aries demands. But all medications can affect the performance of the horse, he adds, so where does the treatment end and the drugging begin?

The authorities reply: a few hours before the race. But Aries says many drugs have a lingering effect, especially if administered in capsules or suppositories, and innocent use may implicate the trainer while guilty use may escape detection.

While the puncture of a needle may produce a telltale bump or spot, Aries reports, drugs may be administered with food or water, in pills and suppositories, and even by massage. The only problem for the drugger, he says, is seclusion.

Drugging, Dr. Aries declares, is a crime without a corpus delicti.

SALIVA TEST DISCOUNTED

In the face of modem drugs, he asserts, the saliva test is a travesty. Most laboratories "are lamentably archaic," and incapable of detecting the new drugs. Further, Aries says, only the winner is tested in most countries, whereas it is reported that drugged horses run in second and third more often than first.

And in Britain, according to one citation, drugging is used more often to make a horse lose than to make it win. Aries observes that this is generally done by parties unfriendly to the stable, since the trainer doesn't need drugs — he can make the horse lose by making it eat or drink before a race, keeping it awake the night before or simply "whispering a few words in the jockey's ear."

What is needed, Aries says, is the application of microanalytic technology just as sophisticated as the technology of drugging. He confesses that even then, convictions would be hard to obtain because the authorities are fearful of scandal and chemists and veterinarians can easily dispute any evidence involving the new drugs.

Nevertheless, he declares, drugging must be stamped out.

Citing Drug Use, Olympic Official Proposes a Ban on Weight Lifting

BY MICHAEL JANOFSKY | SEPT. 30, 1988

SEOUL, SOUTH KOREA, FRIDAY, SEPT. 30 — An Olympic official said Thursday that he would recommend that weight lifting be dropped from future Olympic Games because of drug use by some athletes.

Richard Pound, vice president of the International Olympic Committee, disclosed his plan after a fifth weight lifter was disqualified from the Games for testing positive for a banned drug.

Among eight athletes disqualified at the Olympics after their drug tests produced positive results, five were weight lifters, three of them medal winners.

In addition, the British Olympic Committee acknowledged today that two British athletes, one in track and field, the other in judo, had tested positive. Their names were not released pending testing of their second samples and announcement of any disciplinary action.

Mr. Pound said that he believed the use of steroids was "endemic" among weight lifters and that the international federation governing the sport had not done enough to police their use. As a result, he said he would introduce his proposal at the I.O.C.'s next executive board meeting, in Vienna in December.

"Now may be the time to give weight lifting an Olympic holiday," Mr. Pound said. "There certainly seems to be a problem. Maybe we can take the sport to task, that until they clean themselves up, they can't get back in the Games. It would certainly be a lesson for other sports." He gave no indication as to the length of any ban.

Mr. Pound said that merely placing the proposal to eliminate weight lifting on the agenda at the I.O.C. meeting might increase the weight-lifting federation's vigilance. If not, he said, he was sure the proposal would gain "a fair amount of support."

If the executive board approves the measure in December, it

would be voted upon at a full committee session next year in San Juan, P.R. Tamas Ajan, the general secretary of the International Weight Lifting Federation, said he had been aware of Mr. Pound's feelings for several months.

"I have heard this kind of rumor about Mr. Pound's proposal before," he said. "If he says this kind of statement, I think it would be more fair if we sat down together and discussed the matter."

OFFER OF TESTING DECLINED

As the drug scandals widened, the Canadian track and field squad met and then offered to undergo testing before the Olympics end this weekend. Olympic officials declined to accept their offer, but before they did so, two sprinters — Mark McKoy and Desai Williams — left the team. The two were members of the Canadian 400-meter relay team which, until Ben Johnson's positive test for a steroid and his disqualification, had been a favorite for a medal.

The problems with weight lifting, an Olympic sport since 1928, may be more widespread than the disqualifications indicate.

Steroid use has been viewed as a problem in the sport for some time. Weight lifters have been disqualified from previous international competitions for drug use, but not to the extent to which they have been here.

Dr. Cho Woo Shin, the chief medical officer at the Olympic weight-lifting venue, said that despite the relatively small number of athletes who have tested positive, he suspected that one-fourth to one-third of the lifters competing had used steroids.

DRUG USE IN LOCKER ROOM?

Dr. Cho said lifters might be using drugs even during the competition, in apparent disregard of the possibility they would be caught. He was asked why lifters would risk detection.

"I don't know," he said. "Maybe they underestimate our country's doping capacity or ability."

He said that "two or three times" he had walked into a locker room to see athletes taking what appeared to be drugs. He said he saw one lifter using a syringe. When he approached the lifter, Dr. Cho said, the athlete turned away and tried to conceal his activities.

The other times, Dr. Cho said, he saw athletes ingest a substance.

He said he could not determine what the drugs might have been. Nor would he reveal the identities of the athletes or their countries. He did acknowledge that one he saw ingesting something had been among those disqualified.

He mentioned several methods athletes use to avoid drug detection through the urine samples that are analyzed by a local laboratory sanctioned by the International Olympic Committee.

Personal physicians helping athletes during training know how long banned substances remain in the system, he said. Therefore, athletes are counseled when to stop using them in time for the post-competition testing.

THEORY ON MASKING AGENT

Dr. Cho also shared the opinion of other doctors, including Dr. Robert Voy, the chief medical officer for the United States Olympic Committee, that athletes are using a new masking agent to hide traces of steroids in urine samples.

Without knowing what the agent is, I.O.C. medical laboratories cannot test for it. But Dr. Robert Dugal of Canada, a member of the I.O.C. medical commission, said he did not believe such an agent existed.

When told of Dr. Cho's experiences in the locker room, Dr. Voy said he was not surprised.

"It's just an example of how cavalier the sport has become," he said. "I've heard of athletes who use their own steroids and give themselves their own shots."

The use of banned substances exploded into the forefront of the Olympics earlier this week when Johnson, the Canadian sprinter who had set a world record in winning the 100-meter dash, was found to have used the anabolic steroid stanozolol. He was disqualified from the Games and stripped of his medal.

FIFTH LIFTER DISQUALIFIED

To that point in the Games, six other athletes had been disqualified for positive tests, two of them gold-medal winners in weight lifting from Bulgaria. After they were cited, the entire team withdrew.

Today, a fifth weight lifter, Andor Szanyi of Hungary, the silver medalist in the 220-pound division, was disqualified after testing positive for a steroid.

The other two athletes, besides Mr. Johnson, to test positive at the Games were competitors in the modern pentathlon from Spain and Australia. One was found to have excessive amounts of caffeine in his system.

In the Olympics, the top four finishers in individual events, plus one athlete chosen randomly (two others in weight lifting), are tested for the presence of any of more than 100 banned substances, including steroids, the drug of choice for many athletes in events in which strength is valued. Steroids increase muscle mass and enable an athlete to train harder, and can speed recovery from some injuries.

Two of the disqualified weight lifters took steroids; the other two took diuretics, which hasten weight loss or mask steroid use.

Mr. Pound said he believed the use of drug use by weight lifters was "systemic by countries."

"The coaches and the team doctors, they all deny that it is going on," he said. "But they know that it is."

Olympic Cover-Up?

BY THE NEW YORK TIMES | JUNE 4, 1989

DID THE HEAD of the International Olympic Committee want to suppress the laboratory finding that Ben Johnson had steroids in his system when he set a world record in winning the 100-meter dash at the 1988 Summer Olympics? Johnson's doctor, Jamie Astaphan, testified at a Canadian inquiry last week that he had been told just that. He said he had been told that the I.O.C. president, Juan Antonio Samaranch, would have intervened to prevent the test results from being made public if the laboratory had not leaked the results.

Yesterday, Samaranch responded, denouncing Astaphan's "untruthful statements," insisting that the decision by the I.O.C. executive commission to suspend Johnson had been unanimous and suggesting that a cover-up would have been impossible in any event since more than 30 people knew the results.

In an interview in La Suisse, a Geneva newspaper, Samaranch indicated that Astaphan was indulging in sour grapes. "This doctor is a true doping professional," he said, "and wanted me to pay for my declaration that although an athlete who takes drugs is to be condemned, the real guilty people are to be found in his or her immediate entourage."

In German Courthouse: Pain, Doping, Medals

BY ROGER COHEN | MAY 11, 2000

HE IS A SHRUNKEN MAN these days, his eyes evasive behind glasses. But for more than a quarter-century, Manfred Ewald was little short of a demigod, the undisputed "Sportfuhrer" presiding over Communist East Germany's extraordinary gold-medal machine.

That success, out of proportion with what was a country of 17 million people, has brought Ewald, 75, to a Berlin court. He is charged with administering anabolic steroids to 142 female athletes, who were not told what they were taking and have since suffered symptoms ranging from infertility to a deepening of their voices.

The trial, which began last week, is not the first attempt to judge what the German singer and anti-Communist dissident Wolf Biermann once called "a large-scale animal experiment on living people." But it is the first time that the question of the overall political responsibility for a human experiment that produced 160 gold medals as it severely damaged the bodies of young athletes has come before a court.

Ewald was, over a period of 26 years, a member of the Central Committee of the Communist Party and the man with the political responsibility to produce the Olympic and other medals that would burnish Communism's image in the world. His title was anodyne — President of the East German Gymnastic and Sport Association — but his power enormous.

The indictment — prepared over the past three years by Klaus-Heinrich Debes, a state prosecutor — chronicling how, from 1974, Ewald pursued a program of doping with what the testimony of one Leipzig doctor, Lothar Pickenhain, called "an unbelievable brutality and a merciless heart."

Up to now, during three sessions of the trial, Ewald has declined to testify, and his lawyers have argued that his psychological state is now too fragile for him to appear in court.

But he has in the past been robust in his dismissal of the accusations and is well-known for a blunt, if not quite relevant and plainly questionable, assertion: "Communists do not murder people."

The trial will resume next week after Ewald undergoes psychological tests at a Berlin hospital. Already, his co-defendant, Manfred Hoppner, 66, a doctor who headed the so-called "Working Group on Supporting Means," has been more forthcoming. "Supporting Means" was the official East German euphemism for doping.

"I do not deny that I promoted the application of supporting drugs," Hoppner said in a prepared statement. But he added, "The promotion and medical support of competitive sport did not contradict the laws of East Germany."

The courts of a united Germany have tended to show little sympathy for such pleadings: the exaltation of obedience and duty over conscience and humanity has already brought too much ruin on this country during its modern history.

Certainly, it seems clear that, far from being against the law, the doping for which Ewald was politically responsible was actively supported by the state. The indictment describes how some 30,000 people worked under him and how scarce hard currency was made available to support the program.

For example, he was given $159,000 in 1976 to secure a retreat at the Montreal Olympics that was deemed remote enough to lessen the chances of doping checks.

"I am absolutely sure that as far as the majority of athletes was concerned, the proper use of supporting drugs proved worthwhile," Hoppner argued in court. "As for the athletes who suffered disastrous consequences, I ask them to accept my apology."

But there was little hint of charity from those whose lives were permanently changed. Of the 142 women named, 40 developed deeper voices, 21 suffered an excessive growth of bodily hair, 15 incurred gynecological problems including infertility or miscarriages, six saw their breasts disappear, and others suffered symptoms including the development of outsized muscles.

"We were vehicles chosen to prove that socialism was better than capitalism," said Carola Beraktschjan, 38, a former gold medalist in the 1977 European swimming championships. "What happened to our bodies was entirely secondary to that political mission led by Ewald."

One of the 142 people named in the case, Beraktschjan recalled how she was 13 years old when officials started giving her pills in 1975 that were described as "vitamins" and "minerals." Her first suspicion arose a year later, just before the Montreal Olympics, when she became ill with a liver complaint.

But the following year, she agreed to injections of further "vitamins" and "minerals."

"We were very young," she said, "and you have to understand how helpless we felt."

At the age of 15, the program bore fruit when she secured her European title in the 100-meter breast stroke — a medal she has since returned because she can no longer accept how it was won.

In 1978, as her muscles suddenly swelled and she began to rapidly put on weight, Beraktschjan rebelled and refused to take any more of the substances. She now credits this decision with saving her from the more extreme problems suffered by other women. She has a healthy 13-year-old daughter.

Until recently, however, Beraktschjan had recurrent nightmares about swimming, usually about drowning or being unable to reach the side of the pool. "They were dreams of fear, the fear I carried in me then," she said.

The dreams stopped two years ago after she sought psychological help and witnessed the trial of her former swimming coach, Rolf Gleser, who was fined and given a suspended sentence.

"Now, when I see Mr. Ewald, I feel anger," she said. "But it's not the same direct anger as with my trainer. It's subtler than that, a satisfaction that the mastermind of it all will at last get his due."

Just what, if anything, that due will be remains unclear for now. Sentences in previous doping trials have been light with a 15-month suspended jail sentence among the most severe punishments. But the prosecution is arguing that the responsibility of the "Sportfurher" for medal production is of a different nature from men like Gleser. A verdict is expected later this month.

Drugs Pervade Sport in Russia, World Anti-Doping Agency Report Finds

BY REBECCA R. RUIZ | NOV. 9, 2015

GENEVA — Members of Russia's secret service intimidated workers at a drug-testing lab to cover up top athletes' positive results. They impersonated lab engineers during the Winter Olympics in Sochi last year. A lab once destroyed more than 1,400 samples.

Athletes adopted false identities to avoid unexpected testing. Some paid to make doping violations disappear. Others bribed the antidoping authorities to ensure favorable results, and top sports officials routinely submitted bogus urine samples for athletes who were doping.

Those allegations were among hundreds contained in a report released Monday by the World Anti-Doping Agency. Across 323 pages, it implicates athletes, coaches, trainers, doctors and various Russian institutions, laying out what is very likely the most extensive state-sponsored doping program since the notorious East German regime of the 1970s.

In addition to providing a granular look at systematic doping, the group that drafted the report made extraordinary recommendations, including a proposal that Russia be suspended from competition by track and field's governing body and barred from track and field events at next summer's Olympics in Rio de Janeiro.

"It's worse than we thought," Dick Pound, founding president of the World Anti-Doping Association and an author of the report, said at a news conference in a Geneva hotel. "This is an old attitude from the Cold War days."

Russian officials responded with defiance, disputing the investigation's findings. "Whatever we do, everything is bad," Vitaly Mutko, Russia's sports minister, told the news agency Interfax. "If this whole system needs to shut down, we will shut it down gladly. We will stop paying fees, stop funding the Russian antidoping agency, the Moscow antidoping laboratory. We will only save money."

Dr. Grigory Rodchenkov, the director of the Moscow lab whom Monday's report accused of having solicited and accepted bribes, dismissed the suggestions. "This is an independent commission which only issues recommendations," he said. "There are three fools sitting there who don't understand the laboratory."

Mr. Pound said he had presented the group's findings to Mr. Mutko before they were released publicly. "He's frustrated to some degree," he said. "He certainly knew what was going on. They all knew."

The report also recommended that the World Anti-Doping Agency impose lifetime bans on five Russian coaches and five athletes, including the gold and bronze medalists in the women's 800 meters at the 2012 London Olympics.

"The Olympic Games in London were, in a sense, sabotaged by the admission of athletes who should have not been competing," the report read.

Bans from competition are not all that could come of the inquiry. Mr. Pound said the agency had negotiated a cooperation agreement with Interpol and had handed over extensive documents and evidence. Interpol confirmed that cooperation with its own announcement on Monday, noting that related inquiries stretched from Singapore to France.

Last week, the French authorities announced that they had opened a criminal investigation into the former president of track and field's world governing body, Lamine Diack of Senegal, over allegations that he accepted bribes to allow at least six Russian athletes to participate in competitions, including the 2012 Olympics.

The former director of the medical and antidoping division of that governing body, the International Association of Athletics Federations, is also under investigation, the French authorities said, along with Mr. Diack's legal adviser.

Russian athletes, in soaring numbers, have been caught doping in recent years. Russia had far more drug violations than any other country in 2013 — 225, or 12 percent of all violations globally, according to data from the World Anti-Doping Agency. About a fifth of Russia's infractions involved track and field athletes, the focus of Monday's report.

"This level of corruption attacks sport at its core," Richard H. McLaren, a Canadian lawyer and an author of the report, said in an interview Sunday. In contrast to corporate governance scandals like those currently affecting world soccer, he said, drug use by athletes has distorted the essence of professional games. "Bribes and payoffs don't change actual sporting events," Mr. McLaren said. "But doping takes away fair competition."

The report released Monday was the result of a 10-month investigation by an independent commission of WADA. Its inquiry stemmed from a December 2014 documentary by the German public broadcaster ARD, which drew on accounts from Russian athletes, coaches and antidoping officials, who said that the Russian government had helped procure drugs for athletes and cover up positive test results.

Further allegations emerged in August, when ARD and The Sunday Times of London released another report more broadly covering the leaked results of thousands of international athletes' blood tests dating to 2001, showing decorated athletes in good standing with suspicious drug tests. Those allegations — which drew significant suspicion to Kenya — are also being investigated by the independent commission, but the results were not included in Monday's report, as the inquiry is not complete, the agency said.

The three-person commission, led by Mr. Pound, also included Mr. McLaren, who teaches law at the University of Western Ontario, and Günter Younger, the head of cybercrime for the police in the German state of Bavaria.

WADA's foundation and executive board will decide whether to act on the commission's recommendations; they are scheduled to meet next week in Colorado Springs, an event that motivated the timing of the release of the commission's report, Mr. Pound said.

In a statement on Monday, the International Olympic Committee called the report "deeply shocking" and said it trusted the judgment of the I.A.A.F., which would decide whether to bar Russia from competition.

Mr. Pound did not offer any time frame for the recommended suspension. If Russia did not fight the prescriptions — to enact rigorous and specific drug-testing controls — he said he thought it could be possible for the country's track and field athletes to compete in the Summer Olympics.

"If they do the surgery and do the therapy, I hope they can get there," he said. "That is your nuclear weapon. Either get this done or you are not going to Rio."

The commission also recommended that the Russian antidoping authority be declared non-code-compliant indefinitely; that the director of the Moscow laboratory be removed from his job; and that the lab, which was provisionally banned in 2013, lose its accreditation.

In the case of financial prizes awarded to athletes with drug test results now thought to be tainted, "the money's gone," Mr. Pound said, "and whoever ought to have won didn't."

The Russian Ministry of Sport did not immediately respond to a request for comment. But the initial reaction in Russia fell in line with the tradition since Soviet times, with many attributing the revelations to a Western plot to undermine the country's accomplishments.

"It is all connected with the fact that Russian athletes demonstrate such good results, some countries are not satisfied with it," said Igor Ananskikh, a member of the youth policy and sports committee of the Russian Parliament.

Nikolai Valuev, a former Russian heavyweight boxing champion now serving as a deputy in the Parliament, said on the state-run Rossiya 24 television channel: "In recent times, I hear only about investigations of Russian athletes. This has already become a system, too.

"First of all," he said, "we must conduct a broad investigation to find out whether the results of the investigation are true."

Days before Monday's report was published, however, Russia's athletics federation suspended five athletes, including a noted distance runner, Maria Konovalova.

"The Russians themselves have said there are vestiges of the old Soviet system, old-guard coaches who haven't changed and can't change," Mr. McLaren said. "The minister of sport says their way of operating is over. But read our report."

Russia has had a particularly prominent place in the international sports spotlight in recent years, hosting not only the Winter Games in Sochi in 2014 but also the track and field world championships in Moscow the year before.

The country is scheduled to host the next World Cup, in 2018, although the Swiss authorities are investigating allegations that Russia might have secured the tournament through under-the-table agreements. The Moscow laboratory implicated in Monday's report is set to oversee testing for FIFA during the World Cup. The lab did not immediately respond to a request for comment.

Mr. Pound declined to say whether he thought Russia should be stripped of its status as host of that tournament. "I think FIFA's got to sort out its own difficulties — without our help," he said.

Mr. Mutko, Russia's sports minister, sits on FIFA's executive committee.

"The credibility of sport has taken some serious body blows in the last month," Mr. Pound said, referring to the FIFA corruption case and to Monday's report, which suggested that similar doping violations existed beyond track and field. "Public opinion is going to move toward all sports being corrupt."

Russian Insider Says State-Run Doping Fueled Olympic Gold

BY REBECCA R. RUIZ AND MICHAEL SCHWIRTZ | MAY 12, 2016

LOS ANGELES — Dozens of Russian athletes at the 2014 Winter Olympics in Sochi, including at least 15 medal winners, were part of a state-run doping program, meticulously planned for years to ensure dominance at the Games, according to the director of the country's antidoping laboratory at the time.

The director, Grigory Rodchenkov, who ran the laboratory that handled testing for thousands of Olympians, said he developed a three-drug cocktail of banned substances that he mixed with liquor and provided to dozens of Russian athletes, helping to facilitate one of the most elaborate — and successful — doping ploys in sports history.

It involved some of Russia's biggest stars of the Games, including 14 members of its cross-country ski team and two veteran bobsledders who won two golds.

In a dark-of-night operation, Russian antidoping experts and members of the intelligence service surreptitiously replaced urine samples tainted by performance-enhancing drugs with clean urine collected months earlier, somehow breaking into the supposedly tamper-proof bottles that are the standard at international competitions, Dr. Rodchenkov said. For hours each night, they worked in a shadow laboratory lit by a single lamp, passing bottles of urine through a hand-size hole in the wall, to be ready for testing the next day, he said.

By the end of the Games, Dr. Rodchenkov estimated, as many as 100 dirty urine samples were expunged.

None of the athletes were caught doping. More important, Russia won the most medals of the Games, easily surpassing its main rival, the United States, and undermining the integrity of one of the world's most prestigious sporting events.

"People are celebrating Olympic champion winners, but we are

TONY CENICOLA/THE NEW YORK TIMES

The director of Russia's antidoping laboratory at the time of the Sochi Games said urine samples were surreptitiously replaced by somehow breaking into supposedly tamper-proof bottles.

sitting crazy and replacing their urine," Dr. Rodchenkov said. "Can you imagine how Olympic sport is organized?"

After The New York Times asked Russian officials to respond to the claims, Russia's sports minister, Vitaly Mutko, released a statement to the news media calling the revelations "a continuation of the information attack on Russian sport."

Dr. Rodchenkov laid out the details of the operation over three days of interviews that were arranged by an American filmmaker, Bryan Fogel, who is working on a documentary that involves Dr. Rodchenkov.

Dr. Rodchenkov's account could not be independently verified, but it was consistent with the broad findings of a report published last year by the World Anti-Doping Agency. He provided The Times with emails detailing doping efforts and a spreadsheet that he said was sent to him by the sports ministry before the Sochi Games. It named the athletes involved in the doping program.

Dr. Rodchenkov described his own work at Sochi as a "strong accomplishment," the apex of a decade-long effort to perfect Russia's doping strategy at international competitions.

"We were fully equipped, knowledgeable, experienced and perfectly prepared for Sochi like never before," he said. "It was working like a Swiss watch."

After Sochi, Dr. Rodchenkov was awarded the prestigious Order of Friendship by President Vladimir V. Putin.

Six months ago, however, he had a dramatic change in fortune. In November, the World Anti-Doping Agency identified Dr. Rodchenkov as the linchpin in what it described as an extensive state-sponsored doping program in Russia, accusing him of extorting money from athletes — the only accusation he denies — as well as covering up positive drug tests and destroying hundreds of urine samples.

After the report came out, Dr. Rodchenkov said, Russian officials forced him to resign. Fearing for his safety, he moved to Los Angeles, with the help of Mr. Fogel.

Back in Russia, two of Dr. Rodchenkov's close colleagues died unexpectedly in February, within weeks of each other; both were former antidoping officials, one who resigned soon after Dr. Rodchenkov fled the country.

The November report was primarily focused on track and field, but Dr. Rodchenkov described the whole spectrum of Russian sport as tainted by banned substances. Admitting to more than what WADA investigators accused him of, he said it was not hundreds of urine samples that he destroyed but rather several thousand in last-ditch efforts to mask the extent of the country's doping.

Dr. Rodchenkov said he received the spreadsheet naming athletes on the doping program on Jan. 21, 2014, two weeks before the Games and shortly after he arrived in Sochi to begin work at the Olympic laboratory. It was to be used for reference during competition, Dr. Rodchenkov said, and outlined the competition schedule for each athlete. If any of them won a medal, their urine samples had to be substituted.

Until now, a precise accounting of how Russian officials could have executed such a complex doping operation was not publicly known.

PRESSURE TO WIN

Dr. Rodchenkov's revelations, his first public comments since fleeing, come at a crucial moment for Russia. In November, in the wake of the WADA report, the country was provisionally suspended from international track and field competition; in the coming weeks, leaders of the sport's global governing body will decide whether to lift a ban ahead of this summer's Olympics in Rio de Janeiro.

Russia is also preparing to host the next World Cup, in 2018.

Responding to the cascade of accusations, Mr. Putin called for an inquiry, but Russian officials have been largely dismissive of claims about widespread doping by the country's athletes.

The Times submitted questions about the revelations to the sports ministry and six of its sports federations whose athletes were identified as part of the doping program. Instead of responding directly, Mr. Mutko, the minister, organized a news conference with journalists from the state-run news agency TASS, calling The Times's inquiry baseless and suggesting it was part of an attempt to discredit Russian sports ahead of the Rio Games.

"The system of organization of the Olympic Games was completely transparent," Mr. Mutko told TASS. "Everything was under the control of international experts — from the collection of samples to their analysis."

Dr. Rodchenkov said the sports ministry actively guided the doping effort. In the six months before the Games, he said, he met with Mr. Mutko's deputy, Yuri Nagornykh, in a second-floor office at the ministry's palatial Moscow headquarters at least once a week.

In an email, Mr. Nagornykh denied the existence of a doping program. "I have nothing to hide," he wrote.

Russian officials were under enormous pressure ahead of the Games. Sochi was to be a showcase of Russia's resurgence as a global power, and the entire country was enlisted in the project. Billions of dollars were spent transforming the shabby subtropical resort town into a winter sports paradise. Mr. Putin himself had negotiated Russia's Olympic bid and was personally involved in much of the planning.

Hanging over everything was Russia's disastrous sixth-place finish in the medal count at the previous Winter Olympics, in Vancouver, British Columbia. It would not matter if the world was wowed by the opening ceremony, or if the ski lifts ran smoothly.

Dr. Rodchenkov said it was up to him to ensure that Russian athletes won the most medals, preferably gold ones.

He had been the director of Russia's antidoping laboratory in Moscow since 2005, and was widely considered among the world's top experts in performance-enhancing drugs. He often experimented with such drugs on himself, he said.

He published papers in peer-reviewed journals, traveled often to scientific conferences abroad and was a frequent guest at the annual antidoping symposium organized by the United States Anti-Doping Agency, most recently in October in Lansdowne, Va., just a month before he was forced to step down.

By his own admission, Dr. Rodchenkov, who has a Ph.D. in analytical chemistry, used his expertise to help athletes properly use banned substances and go undetected, which he says was done at the behest of the Russian government. After years of trial and error, he said, he developed a cocktail of three anabolic steroids — metenolone, trenbolone and oxandrolone — that he claims many top-level Russian athletes used leading up to the London Olympics in 2012 and throughout the Sochi Games.

He said he did not administer the drugs himself but rather provided them to the sports ministry.

The drugs, Dr. Rodchenkov said, helped athletes recover quickly after grueling training regimens, allowing them to compete in top form over successive days.

To speed up absorption of the steroids and shorten the detection window, he dissolved the drugs in alcohol — Chivas whiskey for men, Martini vermouth for women.

Dr. Rodchenkov's formula was precise: one milligram of the steroid mixture for every milliliter of alcohol. The athletes were instructed to swish the liquid around in their mouths, under the tongue, to absorb the drugs.

In the interviews, Dr. Rodchenkov boasted about his ability to shield doped athletes from detection. Even so, Russia had the highest number of athletes caught doping in 2014, according to WADA statistics.

Dr. Rodchenkov said that some of his athletes would at times take drugs he had not approved, making them vulnerable to discovery. "All athletes are like small children," he said. "They'll put anything you give them into their mouths."

A case in point, he said, was Elena Lashmanova, a gold medalist in racewalking at the 2012 London Games. She had tested positive for banned substances while international observers were scrutinizing his lab, and to cover up her results would have endangered the entire operation, he said.

In an email to Mr. Nagornykh, the deputy sports minister, dated April 18, 2014, he wrote that there was nothing he could do to protect Ms. Lashmanova without risking the lab's accreditation.

"Honestly, this lawlessness has reached its logical conclusion," he wrote. "There can be no second opinion about this."

Three months later, Ms. Lashmanova was suspended from international competition for two years.

PLANNING FOR SOCHI

For Dr. Rodchenkov, preparations for Sochi began in earnest in the fall of 2013. It was around that time, he said, that a man he came to believe was working for the Russian internal intelligence service, the F.S.B., began showing up at the lab in Moscow, inquiring about the bottles used for storing the urine samples tested for banned substances.

The man took a particular interest in the toothed metal rings that lock the bottles when the cap is twisted shut. He collected hundreds of them, Dr. Rodchenkov said.

An employee at the lab, who spoke only on condition of anonymity, fearing reprisals from the authorities, said that at some point it was communicated to employees that the man was there to "protect the lab." He would pepper people with questions about the bottles, the employee said, but always in a friendly way. While his motivations were not explicit, they eventually became obvious to those working in the lab.

"It was clear that he was going to try to get into the bottles," the employee said.

At all major international athletic competitions, athletes are required to submit a urine sample for testing. The sample is divided into two bottles. One, the A bottle, is tested immediately; the other, the B bottle, is sealed and stored for up to 10 years, in case the athlete's past performance is ever called into question. A Swiss company, Berlinger, produces the self-locking glass bottles used for international competitions, including the Olympics.

Because of the strict testing protocols at competitions, Dr. Rodchenkov said, athletes typically have to halt the use of banned substances before an event to avoid testing positive. But in hosting the Sochi Games, national sports officials saw an opportunity: They could control the antidoping lab results, he said, and allow athletes to use performance-enhancing drugs throughout competition.

Getting into the bottles was the key.

How exactly this was accomplished is still a mystery. Dr. Rodchenkov claims that at some point several weeks before the start of the Games, the man he believed to be an F.S.B. agent presented him with a previously sealed bottle that had been opened, its uniquely numbered cap intact.

"When I first time saw that bottle is open, I did not believe my eyes," he said, adding: "I truly believed this was tamper proof."

SWAPPING OUT DIRTY URINE

In the months before Sochi, according to the November WADA report, international doping officials had threatened to revoke the accreditation of Dr. Rodchenkov's lab because of suspicious discrepancies in sample results and complaints of "external interferences" in the lab's operations. In November 2013, a disciplinary committee convened in Johannesburg to review the case.

"Despite the substandard performance of the laboratory, there was a distinct desire not to revoke the accreditation of the laboratory prior to the Sochi Olympics," last year's WADA report said.

The testing laboratory for the Sochi Games had a staff of nearly 100 people, including employees of Dr. Rodchenkov's lab in Moscow as well as dozens of international antidoping experts, flown in from cities like Beijing; Doha, Qatar; and Lausanne, Switzerland.

Security was tight. There were numerous surveillance cameras, and anyone wishing to enter the lab required security clearance.

An independent observer watched over the lab at random times of day, WADA said, but rarely worked overnight during the roughly two weeks of competition.

Dr. Rodchenkov said that each night, a sports ministry official would send him a list of athletes whose samples needed to be swapped. To match the individual athletes to their anonymous samples — which are coded with a seven-digit number — Dr. Rodchenkov said that athletes snapped pictures of their sample forms, including the code, and texted them to the ministry, offering forbidden insight into whose urine was whose.

After receiving a signal that "the urines were ready," he changed from his lab coat into a Russian national team sweatshirt and left his fourth-floor office, typically after midnight. He checked that the coast was clear and made his way to Room 124, officially a storage space that he and his team had converted into a shadow laboratory.

There, he said, with the room's single window blacked out with tape, the switch would be made.

A colleague stationed next door in the sample collection room would retrieve the correct bottles and pass them into the storage room through a circular hole cut through the wall near the floor, Dr. Rodchenkov said. During the day, he said, the hole was concealed by a small imitation-wood cabinet.

The sealed B bottles were handed over to the man Dr. Rodchenkov believed was a Russian intelligence officer, who would take them to an adjacent building. Within hours, Dr. Rodchenkov said, the bottles were returned to the storage room, their caps unlocked.

That man also supplied clean urine, collected from each of the athletes months prior to the Olympics, before they started doping, Dr. Rodchenkov said. It was delivered in soda bottles, baby formula bottles and other miscellaneous containers, he said.

Making sure to keep the overhead light off, Dr. Rodchenkov and a colleague dumped the tainted urine into a nearby toilet, washed out the bottles, dried them with filter paper and filled them with the clean urine.

He would then add table salt or water to balance out any inconsistencies in the recorded specifications of the two samples. Depending on what an athlete had consumed, two urine samples taken at different times could vary.

Typically, the small team worked till dawn, breaking only occasionally for instant coffee and cigarettes.

VICTORY

In the Sochi Games, Russian athletes won 33 medals — including 13 golds, 10 more than at the previous Winter Olympics.

A third of all medals were awarded to athletes whose names appeared on the spreadsheet outlining the government's doping plan that Dr. Rodchenkov said was provided by the sports ministry before the Games.

They included Alexander Zubkov, a veteran bobsledder who won two golds; Alexander Legkov, a cross-country skier who won gold and silver; and Alexander Tretyakov, who won gold in the skeleton competition.

Still, not all athletes on the list won a medal. The entire women's hockey team was doping throughout the Games, Dr. Rodchenkov said. It finished in sixth place.

Efforts to reach these athletes and others through their sports federations in Russia were unsuccessful. Several of the federations replied and denied any wrongdoing by their athletes. A spokesperson for the Russian Bobsled Federation said that all of its athletes "underwent doping control procedures in accordance to the rules."

"All of them were clean, and not one positive result was found."

The International Olympic Committee called Dr. Rodchenkov's account "very detailed and very worrying" on Thursday. "We ask the

CHANG W. LEE/THE NEW YORK TIMES

Alexander Legkov, a cross-country skier, is among the Olympic champions listed on a spreadsheet, provided by the sports ministry before the Sochi Games, that outlined the government's doping plan, Dr. Rodchenkov said.

World Anti-Doping Agency to investigate immediately," a spokesman said.

WADA officials were in board meetings on Thursday and unavailable for interviews. The agency had previously said it was looking into allegations of Russian doping and the Sochi lab and did not add anything further by email.

SOUTHERN CALIFORNIA

After the Olympics, the praise directed at Dr. Rodchenkov was effusive. He received commendations from not only Mr. Putin, but also the International Olympic Committee and the World Anti-Doping Agency.

A subsequent report published by WADA called Sochi "a milestone in the evolution of the Olympic Games antidoping program."

The next year, however, WADA published a very different report which said investigators had found systematic doping among Russian track and field athletes. That inquiry, prompted by accusations from two whistle-blowers in Russian athletics — first published by the German public broadcaster ARD — put Dr. Rodchenkov squarely at the center of a national conspiracy.

Within days, he was forced to resign, he said, and fearing for his safety, fled to Los Angeles. His travel was arranged by Mr. Fogel, whom he had first met just after Sochi, in 2014. Mr. Fogel was working on a documentary seeking to expose shortcomings in drug-testing for international sport — charting his own competition results with and without banned drugs — and Dr. Rodchenkov served as his adviser.

In his six months in Los Angeles, Dr. Rodchenkov has taken on a more active role in that documentary, "Icarus," to be released in September. He has otherwise spent his time gardening, making borscht and writing in his diary.

Reflecting on his career, he said he was unapologetic about his role in Russia's doping program, considering it a condition of his employment. To receive funding and support for his lab, he said, he had to do the Kremlin's bidding.

He had occasionally, however, run afoul of the Russian authorities in his work. In 2011, he was investigated for trafficking in performance-enhancing drugs, and he said he fully expected to go to prison. His sister was convicted and imprisoned on similar charges.

The investigation into Dr. Rodchenkov, however, disappeared.

He said he could not be sure why, but he suspected that he had been spared punishment so that he could play a crucial role at the Sochi Games.

"It's my redemption: success in Sochi," he said. "Instead of being in prison, win at any cost."

An Olympic Antidoping Champion

OPINION | BY DIONNE KOLLER | JUNE 16, 2016

BALTIMORE — The International Olympic Committee recently announced that 10 refugee athletes from troubled or war-torn nations would be allowed to compete in the summer Olympic Games. The committee believes that the group, officially known as the Refugee Olympic Team, will serve as a "symbol of hope" in Rio de Janeiro.

The I.O.C.'s action to field a refugee team is an example of the Games' spirit at its best — using sport to transcend politics and promote human dignity. The decision also comes at a crucial moment when the Olympic movement's fundamental values seem under attack. Few issues exemplify the crisis more than the allegations of state-supported doping in Russia.

For this reason, the International Olympic Committee and the International Association of Athletics Federations must use their authority to grant a similar special eligibility status to another athlete. In this competitor's case, it is not because she has been forced to flee a conflict zone, but because her moral actions have helped to preserve the integrity of the Olympic movement itself.

That athlete is Yuliya Stepanova, a brave whistle-blower on organized doping in Russian athletics. On Friday in Vienna, an I.A.A.F. task force will report on whether Russia should be permitted to send a track-and-field team to Rio. The panel will also consider whether Ms. Stepanova should be allowed to compete in Rio as an independent competitor, like the refugee athletes.

Ms. Stepanova is an accomplished 800-meter runner from Russia. Because she was a medal contender at the international level, she was, in her words, considered "untouchable." In Russia, that meant an athlete who was doped, with the knowledge of her coaches and sports federation, with performance-enhancing drugs like anabolic

PING ZHU

steroids and the blood-boosting agent EPO, and who was protected from drug-testing controls within her country.

All that changed in 2012. After Ms. Stepanova was injured, the Russian athletics federation stopped protecting her. In 2013, she received a two-year ban from the I.A.A.F. after abnormalities were found in her Athlete Biological Passport, which provides a physiological baseline on every athlete to help identify possible doping.

After much soul-searching, Ms. Stepanova decided to come clean. She chose not to seek a lighter punishment by invoking a provision of the World Anti-Doping Code that permits the World Anti-Doping Agency to reduce sanctions for athletes who provide assistance to antidoping efforts. Instead, she served her ban and joined her husband, Vitaly Stepanov, then an antidoping official, in the risky task of amassing evidence of officially sanctioned Russian doping.

Together, they provided WADA with credible evidence of systemic cheating. Because of their whistle-blowing, the Stepanovs feared for their lives and fled the country, eventually settling in the United States.

Ms. Stepanova has continued to train on her own, returning to competition and earning an Olympic-qualifying time. She has been part of the pool of elite athletes subject to unannounced, out-of-competition testing, and has tested clean. Ms. Stepanova should therefore be considered fully eligible to compete, yet she cannot go home or run for her country.

To maintain its credibility as a proponent of clean sport, the International Olympic Committee must grant Ms. Stepanova the right to compete in Rio independently of Russia. And for the future, the bodies that govern international Olympic competition must establish a new mechanism to protect whistle-blowers like the Stepanovs.

There are currently no rules in the World Anti-Doping Code or the Olympic Charter to protect these vital truth-tellers. The Russian track-and-field scandal could not demonstrate more clearly how much the enforcement of the WADA code in individual countries relies on international governing bodies' ability to protect whistle-blowers.

WADA alone cannot monitor compliance in every country, and the Russian scandal has exposed grave failures in its governance. But relying on each national federation's antidoping efforts is clearly problematic. Some countries, like Britain, Canada and the United States, have antidoping bodies with the funding and political capital to police doping effectively, to test and punish athletes who cheat. But others, like Russia, pay lip service to antidoping measures while fostering a culture of cheating.

As we see from the allegations about how antidoping tests at the 2014 Sochi Winter Olympics were an elaborate charade, it is only through the efforts of principled inside informants like Ms. Stepanova that the truth can come to light. It would make a mockery of the Olympic movement to deny an athlete who has taken enormous personal risks for the cause of clean sport the ability to participate in the Rio Olympics. To do so would, in effect, punish her for speaking the truth and upholding the World Anti-Doping Code and Olympic ideals.

Nearly two decades ago, the establishment of WADA and the adoption of its code were historic steps toward preserving the integrity of clean sport. But Russia's systemic doping has proved the need for further reform. Whistle-blower protections are the logical next step. Granting Ms. Stepanova the right to participate in Rio would go a long way toward ensuring that the Olympics lived up to the ideals of its charter.

The I.O.C.'s generous move in admitting a refugees' team matches the spirit of the Games. So let the committee also extend that grace to a runner who has already proved herself an Olympic champion.

DIONNE KOLLER is a professor at the University of Baltimore School of Law, where she is the director of the Center for Sport and the Law.

Russia Banned From Winter Olympics by I.O.C.

BY REBECCA R. RUIZ AND TARIQ PANJA | DEC. 5, 2017

LAUSANNE, SWITZERLAND — Russia's Olympic team has been barred from the 2018 Winter Games in Pyeongchang, South Korea. The country's government officials are forbidden to attend, its flag will not be displayed at the opening ceremony and its anthem will not sound.

Any athletes from Russia who receive special dispensation to compete will do so as individuals wearing a neutral uniform, and the official record books will forever show that Russia won zero medals.

That was the punishment issued Tuesday to the proud sports juggernaut that has long used the Olympics as a show of global force but was exposed for systematic doping in previously unfathomable ways. The International Olympic Committee, after completing its own prolonged investigations that reiterated what had been known for more than a year, handed Russia penalties for doping so severe they were without precedent in Olympics history.

The ruling was the final confirmation that the nation was guilty of executing an extensive state-backed doping program. The scheme was rivaled perhaps only by the notorious program conducted by East Germany throughout the 1960s, '70s and '80s.

Now the sports world will wait to see how Russia responds. Some Russian officials had threatened to boycott if the I.O.C. delivered such a severe punishment.

President Vladimir V. Putin seemed to predict a boycott of the Pyeongchang Games with a defiant dismissal of the doping scandal and a foreign policy in recent years that has centered on the premise that he has rescued Russia from the humiliation inflicted on it by the West after the collapse of the Soviet Union. His spokesman, Dmitri S. Peskov, said no boycott was under discussion before the announcement, however, and the news broke late in the evening in Moscow when an immediate official reaction was unlikely.

In barring Russia's team, Olympic officials left the door open for some Russian athletes. Those with histories of rigorous drug testing may petition for permission to compete in neutral uniforms. A panel appointed by the International Olympic Committee will rule on each athlete's eligibility.

Although it is unknown exactly how many will clear that bar, it is certain that the contingent from Russia will be depleted significantly. Entire sports — such as biathlon and cross-country skiing, in which Russia has excelled and in which its drug violations have been many — could be wiped out completely.

Olympic officials made two seemingly significant concessions to Russia:

- Any of its athletes competing under a neutral flag will be referred to as Olympic Athletes from Russia. That is a departure from how the I.O.C. has handled neutral athletes in the past. For example, athletes from Kuwait, which was barred from the 2016 Summer Games, were identified as Independent Olympic Athletes last year in Rio de Janeiro
- Olympics officials said they might lift the ban on Russia in time for the closing ceremony, suggesting the nation's flag could make a symbolic appearance in the final hours of the Pyeongchang Games

Thomas Bach, president of I.O.C., has said he was perturbed not only by Russia's widespread cheating but by how it had been accomplished: by corrupting the Olympic laboratory that handled drug testing at the Games, and on orders from Russia's own Olympic officials.

"This decision should draw a line under this damaging episode," Mr. Bach said at a news conference, noting that Alexander Zhukov, the president of Russia's Olympic Committee whom the I.O.C. suspended from its membership Tuesday, had issued an apology — something global regulators have long requested from the nation.

In an elaborate overnight operation at the 2014 Sochi Games, a team assembled by Russia's sports ministry tampered with more than 100 urine samples to conceal evidence of top athletes' steroid use throughout the course of competition. More than two dozen Russian athletes have been disqualified from the Sochi standings as a result, and Olympic officials are still sorting through the tainted results and rescinding medals.

At the coming Games, Mr. Bach said Tuesday, a special medal ceremony will reassign medals to retroactive winners from Sochi. But, in light of legal appeals from many of the Russian athletes who have been disqualified by the I.O.C., it is uncertain if all results from Sochi will be finalized in time.

The Russian Olympic Committee was also fined $15 million on Tuesday, money that global officials said will be put toward drug-testing international athletes.

The punishment announced Tuesday resembles what antidoping regulators had lobbied for leading up to the 2016 Summer Games, where Russia was allowed to participate but in restricted numbers. It is likely to face a legal appeal from Russia's Olympic Committee.

The decision was announced after top International Olympic Committee officials had met privately with Mr. Zhukov; Vitaly Smirnov, Russia's former sports minister who was last year appointed by Mr. Putin to lead a national antidoping commission to redeem Russia's standing in global sports; and Evgenia Medvedeva, a two-time world skating champion.

"Everyone is talking about how to punish Russia, but no one is talking about how to help Russia," Mr. Smirnov said, sipping a hot beverage in the lobby of the Lausanne Palace Hotel before delivering his final appeal to officials. "Of course we want our athletes there, and we want the Russian flag and anthem," he said.

That appeal was rejected in light of the conclusions of Samuel Schmid, a former president of Switzerland whom the Olympic committee appointed last year to review the findings of a scathing investigation commissioned by the World Anti-Doping Agency.

"The analysis is clear and water-tight," Mr. Schmid said Tuesday.

In a 30-page report, he affirmed the credibility of whistle-blowers and investigators who had followed their leads and evidence.

Tuesday's penalty was in line with what had been advocated by two key whistle-blowers whose accounts upended Russia's standing in global sports over the last several years and were cited in Mr. Schmid's report: Grigory Rodchenkov, the chemist who spent 10 years as Russia's antidoping lab chief and was key to carrying out the cheating schemes in Sochi; and Vitaly Stepanov, a former employee of Russia's antidoping agency who married a runner for Russia's national team and was the first to speak publicly about the nation's institutionalized cheating.

"The world knows that hundreds of Olympic dreams have been stolen by the doping system in the country where I was born," Mr. Stepanov wrote in an affidavit submitted to the International Olympic Committee this fall. He had suggested banning Russia's Olympic Committee for two years, or until the nation's antidoping operations are recertified by regulators. Russia and its individual athletes are all but certain to miss the 2018 Paralympics given regulators' refusal to recertify the nation last month.

"The evidence is clear, that the doping system in Russia has not yet been truly reformed," Mr. Stepanov wrote.

Dr. Rodchenkov is living in an undisclosed location in the United States under protection of federal authorities. In August, "Icarus," a film detailing Dr. Rodchenkov's move to the United States and tell-all account, was released. In addition to sworn testimony and forensic evidence, Mr. Schmid cited the film as further evidence in his report.

"Russia's consistent denials lack any credibility, and its failure to produce all evidence in its possession only further confirms its high-level complicity," Jim Walden, a lawyer for Dr. Rodchenkov, said Tuesday. The Russian sports ministry did not immediately respond to a request for comment.

Tuesday's decision could have consequences for another major sports event scheduled to be held in Russia, next year's $11 billion soccer World Cup. The nation's deputy prime minister, Vitaly Mutko, was Russia's top sports official during the 2014 Sochi Games and was directly implicated by Dr. Rodchenkov. As part of Tuesday's ruling, Mr. Mutko was barred for life from the Olympics.

Mr. Mutko is also the chairman of the local organizing committee for the World Cup, but FIFA said in a statement Tuesday that the I.O.C.'s punishments for Olympic doping would have "no impact" on its preparations for the tournament, which begins in June.

CHAPTER 4

The Bigger They Are, the Harder They Fall

The highest tier of athletes — those who capture the attention of the press and the public because of their excellence — find themselves under special scrutiny. The increase of antidoping standards and procedures have exposed doping by some of the most famous athletes. Cyclist Lance Armstrong long denied doping accusations, but overwhelming evidence caused him to come clean, though without making a sincere apology for his behavior. Stars such as Alex Rodriguez did not make the same mistake.

Johnson Loses Gold to Lewis After Drug Test

BY MICHAEL JANOFSKY | SEPT. 27, 1988

BEN JOHNSON OF CANADA, who won the Olympic 100-meter final Saturday in the world-record time of 9.79 seconds, was stripped of his gold medal and today was disqualified from the Games after drug tests showed he had used an anabolic steroid.

The International Olympic Committee announced the test results this morning, and later in the morning, the International Amateur Athletic Federation, the world governing body for track and field, banned Johnson from competition for two years, the maximum penalty. The

Canadian Government banned him for life from receiving a monthly payment he had been receiving from it.

The I.A.A.F. also said that Carl Lewis, who set an American record of 9.92 seconds when he finished second Saturday, would be elevated to the winner's position. Linford Christie of Britain will now get the silver medal, and Calvin Smith of the United States will receive the bronze.

Johnson's positive test is likely to have wide and profound, but quite different, implications for him and for the Olympics.

James Worrall, an I.O.C. member in Canada, said that Johnson "has been killed" as an athlete, and that the sprinter's once-favored status as a hero to many sports fans in Canada, in Jamaica, where he was born, and around the world will now be tarnished.

For the Olympics, however, the finding served as a symbolic victory over those who would cheat to win.

"This is a disaster for Ben, a disaster for the Games, and a disaster for track and field," said Richard Pound, an I.O.C. vice president and a Canadian. "But let's turn this around to make the slate clean and show the world that we do mean business. We are prepared to act, not just to pick out a low-profile athlete in a low-profile sport. If it happens to the best, the same thing will happen."

Worrall said: "If this results in telling every young aspiring athlete, no matter what the sport, that drug-taking just doesn't pay, then perhaps we have achieved something."

Two tests showed that the 26-year-old Johnson had used a substance called stanozolol, a water-based steroid structurally similar to the male hormone testosterone. Johnson was notified of the test results sometime Monday morning, after which he met with I.O.C. officials and representatives of the Canadian Olympic Association. After the meeting, at about 10:30 Monday night, he surrendered his gold medal.

Pound, who attended the meeting, described Johnson as being stunned and said Johnson denied he had used steroids.

'LIKE A TRAPPED ANIMAL'

"He sat there looking like a trapped animal," Pound said. "He had no idea what was going on all around him. He said he didn't do anything wrong and he hadn't taken anything. Sitting there, he was nervous and he could hardly speak."

Charlie Francis, Johnson's coach, also attended the meeting, and Pound described him as being as "equally shocked" as Johnson.

Neither Johnson nor Francis was available for comment. According to some reports, they had left Seoul on a flight to New York.

Substances like stanozolol, one of more than 100 substances banned by the I.O.C., are taken by athletes to increase muscle mass, which in turn enhances their performance. In the Olympics, and most other international and national events, medal winners and other finishers at random are required to give a urine sample after their events.

If an initial test is positive, the I.O.C. medical commission and the athlete's national Olympic committee are notified and a second test is done. If it is also positive, the athlete and his coach are told.

Pound, Worrall and others who know Johnson well held out for the possibility that in some way, Johnson had been manipulated, that he could have been given the steroid without his knowledge or that of his coach, Francis.

In his defense to the Canadian Olympic officials, Johnson and Francis said that Johnson might have been given the substance in a drink sometime before or after the 100-meter final.

Larry Heidebrecht, Johnson's manager, said the positive test was "a mistake or sabotage." He said that Johnson had been given a bottle containing a sports drink at the stadium. Johnson took the bottle back to his living quarters, and that night found what Heidebrecht called "a yellow gooey substance" on the bottom.

Heidebrecht said that Johnson could recall neither when he might have drunk from the bottle nor who gave it to him.

BREACH OF SECURITY

In its deliberations over the I.O.C. Medical Commission recommendation that the test result be accepted, Pound argued on Johnson's behalf that such a scenario could have occurred, and that there might have been a breach of security around the drug-testing operation at the stadium.

But with no hard evidence to substantiate either possibility, the executive board rejected that position, and Pound acknowledged that the chemical analysis of the urine sample had indicated a "chronic suppression of his adrenal functions." That would indicate, he said, that Johnson had been using the steroid for a period of time.

"It was not one offense of ingestion," Pound said.

Prince Alexandre de Merode, the chief of the I.O.C. Medical Commission, said I.O.C. doctors said the test results "excluded all possibility" that the drug could have been administered after the competition and before the test.

In the face of the chemical analysis and their familiarity with Johnson as an athlete and a person, both Pound and Worrall felt that Johnson was an innocent victim of someone.

"Obviously, people behind him, medical people, are responsible," Worrall said. "Ben is a lad who will follow instructions. If he is told that something is good, he will believe it. The whole thing points up the tragedy of the whole system endemic in international sports."

Pound called Johnson "a pawn in this, the host organization for the substance."

The test results would seem to vindicate Lewis, who was criticized last year for saying, after Johnson had defeated him at the world track and field championships in Rome, in the world record time of 9.83 seconds, that some "champions in this meet" had used performance-enhancing drugs.

Lewis did not mention Johnson by name, but the reference to Johnson was unmistakable.

LEWIS HOLDS TO CHARGE

Johnson, who had finished third to Lewis in the Los Angeles Olympics in 1984, had dismissed Lewis's remarks, accusing him of being a poor loser. But in subsequent interviews, Lewis held to his claim.

Today, when informed of developments, Lewis said, "If there is an incident, I am deeply sorry." He declined further comment.

"My obvious reaction to this is one of a degree of total devastation," said Worrall. "If you were looking for an example of the absolute destructive potential of drug taking, this is it."

Worrall then referred to the speech given by Juan Antonio Samaranch, the I.O.C. president, that opened the I.O.C. meetings preceeding the Games.

"He said doping equals death," Worrall said. "Ben Johnson has just been killed as an athlete, and probably his complete life has been ruined."

With Johnson now deposed as champion, Lewis is in a position to win gold medals in the same four events that he won in Los Angeles in 1984. On Monday, he won the long-jump competition. Finals in his other two events, the 200 meters and the 400-meter relay, are scheduled for later in the week.

At Los Angeles in 1984, 12 athletes tested positive for drug use. Through the first 10 days of competition here, seven athletes have tested positive, including the two Bulgarians who won gold medals in weight lifting.

In an interview Monday, Samaranch said that the "only problem" of the Seoul Games had been one of drug use by athletes. He referred to the speeches he had given to open the Calgary Games last winter and these Games. In those speeches, he castigated those athletes who would use drugs and the doctors who would help them find new drugs to use.

"We are showing that the system works," Samaranch said, alluding to the sophisticated testing laboratories, in which 4,000 drugs or more can be detected. "We are showing that my words are not only words, they are facts. We are winning the battle against doping."

Armstrong's Wall of Silence Fell Rider by Rider

BY JULIET MACUR | OCT, 20, 2012

FLOYD LANDIS, the cyclist who had denied doping for years despite being stripped of the 2006 Tour de France title for failing a drug test, went to a lunch meeting in April 2010 with the director of the Tour of California cycling race.

As they sat down at a table at the Farm of Beverly Hills restaurant in Los Angeles, Landis placed a tape recorder between them and pressed record.

Landis finally wanted to tell the truth: He had doped through most of his professional career. He was recording his confessions so he would later have proof that he had blown the whistle on the sport.

"How do you expect people to believe you when you lied for so long?" Andrew Messick, the race director, asked Landis. "Have you told your mother? Have you told Travis Tygart?"

Landis, raised as a Mennonite, said he had not yet told his mother. Nor had he told Tygart, the chief executive of the United States Anti-Doping Agency, with whom he had clashed for more than two years as Landis publicly fought his doping case.

But, Landis said, it was time.

"Lance Armstrong never came up," Messick said in an interview last week. "But he did make a comment on the Mafia. He said, When you're in the Mafia and you get caught and go to jail, you keep your mouth shut, and the organization takes care of your family. In cycling, you're expected to keep your mouth shut when you test positive, but you become an outcast. Everyone just turns their back on you."

Antidoping officials on multiple continents had pursued Armstrong for years, in often quixotic efforts that died at the wall of silence his loyal teammates built around him as the sport's global king. Armstrong kept the dark side of his athletic success quiet, investigators and cyclists said, by using guile and arm-twisting tactics that put fear in those who might cross him.

But the lunch conversation between Landis and Messick would eventually be seen as the first significant crack in Armstrong's gilded foundation, a critical turning point in antidoping officials' quest to penetrate the code of secrecy that endured in cycling.

It set in motion a series of events that led to the stark revelation that Lance Armstrong, the seven-time Tour de France winner, and his United States Postal Service team were engaged in what antidoping officials called the most sophisticated doping program in history — one covered up by cyclists who banded together to protect themselves, one another and the ugly, deceitful underbelly of the sport.

Armstrong, who vehemently denies ever doping, in August stopped fighting the charges the antidoping agency brought against him. Last week, in the wake of antidoping officials' making public their evidence in the case, Armstrong stepped down as the chairman of his cancer foundation and lost nearly all his endorsements — a decline so unceremonious and severe that a precedent in recent sports history is elusive.

On Monday, cycling's world governing body is expected to announce whether it will appeal the antidoping agency's ruling to bar Armstrong for life from Olympic sports, a decision Armstrong has called unfair and flawed. If the group does not appeal, Tour de France organizers will officially strip Armstrong of his Tour titles.

Interviews with more than a dozen riders, their wives, lawyers involved in the case, antidoping officials and team executives revealed that Armstrong's undoing was the culmination of an inquiry that played out over more than two years — but that drastically turned over the course of several weeks this spring as more and more cyclists contributed their own damning stories to the investigation.

At that point, antidoping officials hardly had an airtight case. Tygart was hurriedly approaching cyclists from Armstrong's United States Postal Service teams.

"Look, the system of doping in the sport is coming down, and all the riders, including Lance Armstrong, are going to be given an opportunity to get on the lifeboat," he told them. "Are you on it?"

Rider after rider asked, "Am I going to be the only one?"

It would take months for them to find out.

A FEDERAL INVESTIGATION

The antidoping agency knew its case against Armstrong had the potential to be a blockbuster.

Landis's doping confession and claim that Armstrong and other Postal Service riders were involved in team-organized doping became public in May 2010, at the Tour of California. A federal investigation into Armstrong regarding doping-related crimes, including fraud and drug trafficking, ensued.

The morning after the race ended, David Zabriskie — a five-time national time-trial champion and one of Armstrong's former

CHRISTINE COTTER FOR THE NEW YORK TIMES

Detailed testimony from riders like David Zabriskie helped the United States Anti-Doping Agency's case against Armstrong.

teammates — showed up on the doorstep of the federal courthouse in Los Angeles, finally ready to tell his story. He had requested that Tygart be in the room — he was one of two riders who did so — and what Tygart heard was chilling.

Zabriskie, a gangly rider with a sharp, quirky wit, said he had gone through some bad things in life, but being pushed to use drugs was one of the worst.

The day he first used the banned blood booster erythropoietin, or EPO, he said, Johan Bruyneel — the Postal Service team director and longtime Armstrong confidant — had told him that "everyone is doing it." Hearing that had crushed him.

His father had been an alcoholic, drug user and drug dealer and died young because of it, Zabriskie said Thursday in his first interview since his testimony in Armstrong's case was made public.

His father would push his mother around, prompting the young Zabriskie to step in and try to protect her. One night, when Zabriskie was in junior high, his father was arrested after a SWAT team burst into their suburban Salt Lake City home.

Cycling became a refuge. Bruyneel took Zabriskie under his wing shortly after Zabriskie's father died in 2000 from a failing liver. Soon, he was pressing Zabriskie to use performance-enhancing drugs, Zabriskie said.

"What Johan did to me, I consider it a form of abuse because it was so horrible and affected me for the rest of my life," Zabriskie said, choking up. "I know I was the first person to tell my story because Johan, he doesn't need to be around young cyclists."

Bruyneel has been charged by antidoping officials with administering the doping program on Armstrong's teams. He has consistently denied all doping charges; his case is going to arbitration. He could not be reached for comment.

By the time Zabriskie told his story, Armstrong was trying to keep his former teammates from cracking. He listened in on at least one call his former teammates made to Bruyneel about the investigation, Zabriskie said. He assured his former teammates that everything would be O.K.

In public, he seemed unfazed. After Landis's accusations came out, Armstrong responded indignantly.

"It's just our word against his," he said at the Tour of California. "And we like our word."

Within days, though, unbeknown to Armstrong, that would no longer be true. Zabriskie and at least one other rider had quietly taken Landis's side.

The evidence against Armstrong was mounting, though slowly.

Tygart and the antidoping agency backed off from their investigation while the federal authorities moved ahead. Riders offered their testimony to prosecutors, but some, like Tyler Hamilton and Levi Leipheimer, opened up only when a subpoena for a grand jury compelled them to.

Meanwhile, Armstrong or his representatives worked to wrestle control of the situation. They reached out to former Postal Service riders to offer legal representation, according to lawyers involved in the case.

Early on, George Hincapie, the only rider at Armstrong's side for all seven of his Tour de France victories, retained a lawyer in California, but that lawyer was a fan of Armstrong's and a supporter of his Livestrong charity. Hincapie decided to hire a new lawyer, one based in New York who had no connection with Armstrong, said one person with direct knowledge of the situation.

Hincapie met with federal investigators voluntarily in August 2010 to tell them he had doped and that Armstrong had used blood transfusions, EPO and testosterone.

Armstrong asked Hamilton, one of his former top lieutenants, to enter a joint defense agreement, Hamilton's lawyer said. He sent an e-mail to Michael Barry, a Canadian rider, asking if he would be willing to testify that there was no doping on the Postal Service team, Barry said. Neither said yes.

After Leipheimer testified to the federal grand jury, he said, Armstrong sent his wife a text message saying, "Run, don't walk," which Leipheimer took as a threat.

All those riders kept quiet about their testimony and waited — and waited — to see what would come of it.

A SETBACK

Nothing came of it.

Without explanation, André Birotte Jr., the United States attorney for the Central District of California, dropped the federal inquiry in February, stunning Tygart and the riders and even the investigators involved in the case.

The riders, who believed they had risked their reputations to confess their doping to help shed light on their tarnished sport, were disheartened. Armstrong, who had fought off doping accusations for more than a decade, had won again, some said.

Tygart asked the federal investigators to share some evidence they had uncovered outside the grand jury. But the Justice Department would not comply, he said.

For Tygart, time was running out. The London Olympics were less than three months away, and some of the former Postal Service riders were likely candidates for the United States team. He could not let those riders compete at the London Games if their doping history would soon become public as part of Armstrong's case.

On April 30, Tygart wrote a letter to the Department of Justice, asking for information that he said would "clearly establish that some of the top American cyclists have been involved with doping, and thus should not be allowed to participate in the Olympic Games."

But the Justice Department again left the United States Anti-Doping Agency hanging. More than two years had gone by since Landis broke the silence about the Postal Service team, and the agency's case was languishing.

A MANAGER AND HIS TEAM

The antidoping agency started calling the riders it knew had cooperated with the federal case.

Jonathan Vaughters, a former teammate of Armstrong's and now the team manager of the Garmin-Sharp team, decided that it was time to urge his riders to deliver on a promise.

The night Landis's accusations became public in May 2010, Vaughters had gathered his cyclists in his hotel room in Visalia, Calif., a stop in the Tour of California, and said they should tell the truth if they were contacted by any cycling, antidoping or government authority. He made sure they knew their jobs would be safe.

He knew that Zabriskie, Tom Danielson and Christian Vande Velde — former Postal Service riders — had used performance-enhancing drugs, and he had hired them despite it. Vaughters himself had used performance-enhancing drugs while on the Postal Service team and had once seen Armstrong inject EPO, he said.

As early as 2004, when Tyler Hamilton had tested positive at the Olympics, Vaughters started meeting with the antidoping agency, telling of ways to catch riders who were cheating while only hinting that he had firsthand knowledge of doping.

Vaughters continued working quietly with antidoping officials, waiting for an opportunity to come clean with several others so it would be difficult for Armstrong to dismiss their accusations.

"So I waited and waited," Vaughters said. "It took a whole lot of patience and, frankly, it hurt me a lot over the years to hear people say I was weak for not speaking up. But I was waiting for an opening, and that opening was Floyd."

FLOODGATES OPEN

In the months leading to the Tour of California in 2010, Vaughters said he received increasingly desperate e-mails from Landis, who had just come off his two-year doping suspension and could not find a job in the sport.

Landis was sending Vaughters poetry and Led Zeppelin lyrics that made it clear that he was struggling.

"I felt like he was going to commit suicide or tell all," said Vaughters, who knew the truth about Landis's doping.

PAUL GILHAM/GETTY IMAGES

Travis Tygart, second from left, and the United States Anti-Doping Agency built a case against Armstrong.

Vaughters was right. Less than a week after Landis had lunch with Messick, Landis found himself sitting across from Tygart in a conference room at the Los Angeles airport, telling him everything. He described the doping that occurred while he was on the Postal Service team and said other riders, including Armstrong, Hincapie, Leipheimer and Zabriskie, had doped.

This spring, those and other riders were invited to help the antidoping agency in its investigation. Tygart and Bill Bock, the antidoping agency's general counsel, wanted them to come clean.

"We are here to dismantle the dirty system that still exists in cycling so this won't ever happen to another rider again," Tygart and Bock told them.

Vaughters said their motivation sounded genuine.

"They weren't selling them immunity, like, 'Here's some candy, little girl, come into our van,' " he said. "My guys were going to be honest, no matter what. But it wasn't easy because they had never even told their families."

The riders found Tygart to be a good, honest guy, they said. But Bock, a father of five and summa cum laude graduate of Oral Roberts University, had been particularly convincing and empathetic, they said. When Bock visited Frankie Andreu, a former Postal Service rider, in the spring, Frankie's wife, Betsy, found Bock to be kind and funny, soothing a potentially awkward situation.

"All he ever said was we only want the truth, even if it won't benefit us," she recalled.

Bock, Tygart and the agency's legal affairs director, Onye Ikwuakor, visited rider after rider in May and June, gathering testimonies filled with unimaginable details.

For hours, often with breaks so the riders could regain their composure, the riders confessed their transgressions and others'. Zabriskie talked. Vaughters, Danielson and Vande Velde talked. Even Leipheimer and Hamilton talked.

Among the final witnesses was Hincapie, one of the most respected riders in cycling. Antidoping officials met with him in June, just days before the antidoping agency notified Armstrong of his potential doping violation.

When Hincapie confessed and said Armstrong had doped and encouraged it, the antidoping agency knew it had its case.

Hincapie, Leipheimer, Vande Velde and Zabriskie agreed to take their names out of consideration for the Olympics. They and Danielson agreed to a six-month suspension that would begin Sept. 1, after the cycling season.

In the weeks afterward, Armstrong pressed to know the names of the witnesses, but the antidoping agency would not release them, fearing he would intimidate and silence them before they could testify at an arbitration hearing.

In August, Armstrong gave up. He said he would not continue to fight the charges. The decision sent the antidoping agency scrambling yet again to gather affidavits from the riders who were supposed to provide live testimony at the arbitration hearing. They managed to do so in a little more than three weeks.

At the last minute, the antidoping agency contacted one more cyclist — Michael Barry — because he had recently retired. Barry joined the others and told his doping tale.

"Ultimately, I was living a lie," Barry said last week, adding that he should have been honest from the start, but he felt trapped because he would have lost his job for coming clean.

"I guess I have to apologize to Floyd for calling him a liar," Barry said. "Because he was telling the truth the whole time."

For Armstrong, a Confession Without Explanation

JULIET MACUR | JAN. 17, 2013

THE FORMERLY DEFIANT Lance Armstrong once said, "As long as I live, I will deny ever doping," but sitting face to face with Oprah Winfrey in an interview that was broadcast Thursday, he reversed course.

With Winfrey, he lost his icy stare and buried his cutting words. Looking nervous and swallowing hard several times, he admitted to using through most of his cycling career a cocktail of drugs, including testosterone, cortisone, human growth hormone and the blood booster EPO.

Yet, like always, Armstrong could not help fighting.

He called his doping regimen simple and conservative, rejecting volumes of evidence by the United States Anti-Doping Agency that the drug program on his Tour de France-winning teams was "the most sophisticated, organized and professionalized" doping scheme in the history of cycling.

He said that he was not the kingpin of the doping program on his teams, as the antidoping agency claimed, and that he was just doping the way the rest of his teammates were at the time.

He said he had doped, beginning in the mid-1990s, through 2005, the year he won his record seventh Tour. He said that he took EPO, but "not a lot," and that he had rationalized his use of testosterone because one of his testicles had been removed during his battle against cancer. "I thought, Surely I'm running low," he said of the banned testosterone he took to gain an edge in his performance.

At times during the interview, which will resume Friday night, Armstrong seemed genuinely humble, admitting that he was "a flawed character" and that he would spend the rest of his life trying to apologize to people and regain their trust.

"There will be people who hear this and never forgive me," he said. "I understand that."

But when asked about the people he had tried to crush while he tried to keep his doping secret — people like the former masseuse Emma O'Reilly or his former teammate Frankie Andreu and Andreu's wife, Betsy — he showed little contrition. Those are some of the people who claimed he had doped and who he subsequently publicly claimed were liars. He had called O'Reilly a prostitute and an alcoholic.

In the interview, Armstrong acknowledged calling Betsy Andreu crazy. But with a suggestion of a smirk, he said he never claimed she was fat.

He said he had been a bully his whole life, before contradicting himself a minute later, saying he became a bully only after he survived cancer and resumed his cycling career.

And when he said he never failed a drug test — saying, "I passed them because there was nothing in the system" — he contradicted himself again. When Winfrey asked if his urine samples from the 1999 Tour retroactively tested positive for EPO, he said yes. When she pressed him, he admitted that he received a backdated prescription from a team doctor after he tested positive for cortisone at the 1999 Tour.

Armstrong did not delve into the details of his doping, and Winfrey never asked. He did not explain how it was done, who helped him do it or how, exactly, he perpetuated his myth for so long. He said he was not comfortable talking about other people when asked about the infamous Italian sports doctor Michele Ferrari, his former trainer, who is now serving a lifetime ban for doping his athletes.

When Winfrey asked if he would cooperate with the United States Anti-Doping Agency in building doping cases against others in the sport, he masterfully skirted the question.

Travis Tygart, the chief executive of the antidoping agency, called Armstrong's admission "a step in the right direction."

But it did not really matter what Armstrong told Winfrey in the interview, at least according to Tygart and other antidoping agency officials who hold the key to Armstrong's future as a professional athlete.

Armstrong's reason for coming clean was not to unburden himself of the deception he fought to keep secret for so long. It was to take the first step toward mitigating the lifetime ban from Olympic sports that he received from the United States Anti-Doping Agency in the fall, according to people close to him who did not want their names published because they wanted to stay in Armstrong's good graces.

Antidoping officials need to hear more from Armstrong than just an apology and a rough outline of his doping. They need details. And lots of them.

"Anything he says on TV would have no impact whatsoever under the rules on his lifetime suspension," Tygart said.

Armstrong, 41, wants to compete in triathlons and in running events again, but he is barred from many of those events because they are sanctioned by organizations that follow the World Anti-Doping Code. To get back into those events, he must tell antidoping officials details of who helped him dope, who knew about his doping and who helped him create one of the biggest cover-ups in the history of sports.

In digging up those details, Armstrong might be able to dig himself out of his lifetime ban in exchange for a reduced ban of, perhaps, eight years.

It might also shine the spotlight on some of the most powerful men in the sport of cycling, including Pat McQuaid, the president of the International Cycling Union and a current member of the International Olympic Committee, and Hein Verbruggen, a past president of the cycling union and a current honorary member of the I.O.C.

At least two of Armstrong's teammates have claimed that the cycling union accepted a bribe from Armstrong to cover up at least one positive test. But only a small group of people would be able to prove those claims were true, and Armstrong is one of those people. With Winfrey, Armstrong denied that he had bribed sports officials to hide an alleged positive EPO test at the Tour of Switzerland.

In the end, though, Armstrong seemed to understand that his actions and lies were not normal, even in a sport that was rife with doping during the time he dominated it.

Winfrey asked him if he ever felt his doping was wrong, and he answered no, and then added that he realized that was scary.

When she asked him if he had ever felt bad about his doping, he said no, and then said, "Even scarier."

Winfrey then asked, "Did you feel in any way that you were cheating?"

He said no, "that's the scariest," and went on to explain that he had even looked up the word "cheat" in the dictionary once to find out the exact meaning. He found it to be "gaining an advantage on a rival or foe" and convinced himself that he was not cheating because he considered cycling to be a level playing field then, with all the top riders using drugs.

But throughout Winfrey's interview, Armstrong failed to do the one thing many people had been waiting for: he failed to apologize directly to all the people who believed in him, all the cancer survivors and cycling fans who thought his fairy-tale story was true.

Not once did he look into the camera and say, without qualification, "I'm sorry."

End of the Ride for Lance Armstrong

BY JULIET MACUR | MARCH 1, 2014

THE $10 MILLION ESTATE of Lance Armstrong's dreams is hidden behind a tall, cream-colored wall of Texas limestone and a solid steel gate. Visitors pull into a circular driveway beneath a grand oak tree whose branches stretch toward a 7,806-square-foot Spanish colonial mansion.

The tree itself speaks of Armstrong's famous will. It was once on the other side of the property, 50 yards west of this house. Armstrong wanted it at the front steps. The transplantation cost $200,000. His close friends joke that Armstrong, who is agnostic, engineered the project to prove he didn't need God to move heaven and earth.

For nearly a decade, Lance Armstrong and I have had a contentious relationship. Seven years have passed since his agent, Bill Stapleton, first threatened to sue me. Back then, I was just one of the many reporters Armstrong had tried to manipulate, charm or bully.

I've interviewed him one-on-one in five countries; on team buses that smelled of sweat-soaked Lycra at the Tour de France, in swanky New York City hotel rooms, in the backs of limousines, in soulless conference rooms; and for hours by telephone.

Now, in the spring of 2013, after his whole world has come crashing down and moving trucks are en route to dismantle his beloved estate, I've come to visit him at home in Austin, Tex., for the first time.

Yes, fine, come on out, he said. Troubled by endless obituaries of his celebrated (and now fraudulent) career, he wanted to ensure that I wrote "the true story."

•

John Thomas Neal — a man who would come to know Armstrong better than anyone, better than even Armstrong himself — was an independently wealthy real estate investor and massage therapist, a husband and father, who worked as a soigneur in elite cycling. Soigneur is a French term meaning "one who cares for others." In cycling, that person gives the riders massages, prepares their lunches and water bottles, cleans their uniforms and transports their baggage. A fixer, nurturer and wise counselor, Neal had worked with professional athletes on the beach volleyball tour and with swimmers at the University of Texas. But his passion was cycling because he loved the sport and the travel.

Though he had a law degree, legal work didn't satisfy him and he didn't stick with it. Anyway, he could afford to quit because he had married into money. So in Austin, he volunteered to work with the athletes at the University of Texas. In time, he had made enough connections and had cultivated a reputation in the Olympic sports world for being so good at his job that he was hired as a soigneur for the Subaru-Montgomery professional cycling team. Eddie Borysewicz, a former United States Olympic cycling coach, was in charge of the team, owned by Thomas Weisel, an investment banker who would eventually own the United States Postal Service cycling team.

When he first signed on, Neal worked races only in the United States and hadn't heard much about doping, except that performance-enhancing drug use among cyclists was prevalent in Europe.

He met Armstrong in 1989 at a Texas triathlon, after Borysewicz told him to look out for the budding cycling star. Armstrong's all-out effort at the 1989 junior worlds in Moscow had caught Borysewicz's eye. The coach convinced Armstrong to switch to cycling from triathlon because cycling was an Olympic sport.

Armstrong, perhaps the hottest up-and-coming cyclist in the world, later landed a spot with the Subaru-Montgomery team. By then, Neal and Armstrong knew each other well.

Nearly a dozen athletes in Austin — both men and women — still say they were closer to Neal than to their fathers. He brought them into his family and gave them stability. Armstrong was just the latest athlete in need. Neal also became close friends with Armstrong's mother, Linda.

Armstrong was relocating to Austin from Plano because its hilly terrain was perfect for training. At a steeply discounted rate, Armstrong moved into an apartment complex owned by Neal. Near downtown — among tall trees, 20 paces from Neal's office — it was a comfortable, safe place that Armstrong could call home. Later, Armstrong told The Dallas Morning News his apartment was "killer ... s-o-o-o nice!" He and Neal met every day, sometimes several times a day, for massages and meals. It gave Neal satisfaction to know that he could have a positive impact on a teenager who needed some guidance.

Neal's first impression was that the kid's ego exceeded his talent. Armstrong was brash and ill-mannered, in desperate need of refinement. But the more he learned of Armstrong's home life, the sorrier Neal began to feel for him. He was a boy without a reliable father. Linda Armstrong wrote in her 2005 autobiography that she was pleased that her son had found a responsible male role model, and that Neal had lent a sympathetic ear to her while she dealt with the rocky transition between marriages.

Neal soon recognized that Armstrong's insecurities and anger were products of his broken family: He felt abandoned by his biological father and mistreated by his adoptive one. Armstrong didn't like to be alone, so Neal often met him for breakfast at the Upper Crust Cafe, just down the street from Neal's house, and for lunch at a sports bar called the Tavern. Armstrong ate dinner with the Neals, including their three children, several times a week. It was nothing fancy — sometimes just slow-cooked beans eaten with plastic utensils out of mismatched mugs, as if they were on a camping trip. But they were a family.

Frances, Neal's wife, and Armstrong were the group's jokers. They might chase each other around the dinner table. They might sing parts of "Ice Ice Baby" by the Dallas rapper Vanilla Ice, a song that then sat atop the music charts. One would sing, "Ice ice baby!" and the other would reply, "Too cold, too cold!" On some days, they would bring their show to the Neals' motorboat, where they would spend the day swimming or water-skiing.

It was arguably the happiest, most uncomplicated time in Armstrong's life. He no longer had to worry about his adoptive father, Terry Armstrong, whom he considered overbearing, and his mother's current marital woes were 215 miles north on Interstate 35 in Plano. His world centered on Austin and Neal, who gladly opened his home or apartments to national team cyclists — like Armstrong's future Postal Service teammates George Hincapie, Frankie Andreu, Chann McRae and Kevin Livingston — who wanted to train with Armstrong in the Texas Hill Country.

The day after Armstrong moved into his new apartment, the Neals saw him ride in Lago Vista, 35 miles from Austin. Armstrong did poorly and admitted to Neal that he'd been up late the night before, drinking at an Austin strip club named the Yellow Rose. Neal passed it off as his being just another rambunctious teenager testing his newfound freedom.

•

In 1996, Neal was found to have multiple myeloma, a rare cancer of the plasma cells that inhibits the production of healthy blood cells. Several months later, Armstrong discovered that he had testicular cancer. The two of them grew even closer while enduring chemotherapy together.

In the last two years of Neal's life, from spring 2000 to fall 2002, in hopes of writing a book, he recorded 26 hours of audiotape. The tapes recreate and comment on the most exciting times of his life, primarily the years when the young Lance Edward Armstrong rose from obscurity to superstardom.

Neal, who died of cancer just after Armstrong had survived his bout with the disease, never finished the book. Long after his death, the tapes remained hidden in the bedroom closet of his son, Scott. Nobody in the family had listened to them, but I was given the tapes, along with permission to use Neal's words in this book. While in Austin to transcribe the recordings, I met with Armstrong and asked him about his former best friend.

"J. T. Neal? Forget about that. Don't go chasing that," he told me.

He dismissed Neal's importance, saying Neal hadn't known anything about his doping because his drug use had started after they had grown apart. But in just a few hours, I was sitting in the Neal household, headphones on, listening to the first tape that Neal had recorded.

It brought Neal's voice to life: "Today is the 12th of April, and this is the beginning of my recollections on Lance Armstrong ... "

•

One call from Armstrong to Neal came before dawn in August 1991. Could Neal pick him up in San Marcos? Armstrong wasn't stranded on the side of the road in the Texas outback. He had not blown out a tire on his bike in a marathon training ride. He was in jail.

The night before, 30 miles from Austin, Armstrong had partied with some women from Southwest Texas State University. As they frolicked in an outdoor Jacuzzi at one women's apartment complex, they made so much noise that the police came. But that was only Armstrong's first meeting with officers that night. The second was the big one. Pulled over for driving erratically, he thought he could talk his way out of trouble. So what if he had appeared drunk and refused to take a Breathalyzer test? He was sure the officer would be impressed when he told them who he was: the best young cyclist in the country.

Had he been a quarterback, maybe the ploy would have worked. But a Texas police officer could not care less about a guy's boasting about his prowess on a bike. No, it was off to the county lockup.

Neal, always concerned about Armstrong's drinking and driving, picked him up from the San Marcos jail the next day. Months later, upon receiving a notice that his driver's license could be suspended, Armstrong forwarded it to Neal. On the envelope, he wrote: "J. T. — This came today?? Have a great Xmas! Lance." Now acting as his lawyer as well as his friend, Neal helped Armstrong beat the charges and keep his license.

In turn, Neal received from Armstrong something rare and precious: Armstrong's trust. Armstrong sent him postcards from training trips and races — such as a note dated Aug. 16, 1991, from Wein-und Ferienort Bischoffingen, Germany.

"J. T. — Hows it going? Well, Germany is very nice. As you probably know the worlds are a little over a week away and I'm nervous as hell. At least I'm riding good now! Wish you were here! The boys say 'hello.' Lance"

Neal loved that the national team riders and American pro cyclists knew who he was. Some even called him for advice. In Hincapie's case: I was stopped by customs with a suitcase filled with EPO and other drugs, what should I do? Some of them, like Armstrong and Hincapie, were open with him about their drug use. Whether Neal was complicit in any of their doping is unclear. He said, though, that soigneurs in the United States had a different job from those in Europe, where an intimate knowledge of pharmaceuticals had long been required. Neal learned that from soigneurs who had worked overseas.

According to Neal, Armstrong relied on shots and intravenous drips for recovery and prerace boosts of energy. On the eve of the road race at the 1992 Olympics, fellow cyclist Timm Peddie walked into Armstrong's hotel room and saw Neal and a gaggle of USA Cycling officials standing around Armstrong as he lay on a bed, hooked to an IV.

Peddie was astonished at the openness of the procedure. Everyone there stared at the unexpected guest until Peddie left as quickly as he had come in. He wasn't sure what he had seen. Maybe a blood transfusion? An infusion of electrolytes or proteins? He only knew that he had never received an IV before a race. Armstrong was, evidently, special.

At Christmas 1993, the year Armstrong won a world championship and a million-dollar bonus, Armstrong thanked Neal with several gifts. One was an autographed jersey. In black marker, he signed it: "J. T. I'm very fortunate that our paths have crossed. You're truly my righthand man! Not to mention my best friend! Lance Armstrong."

He gave Neal a Rolex watch inscribed "To J. T. From LANCE ARMSTRONG."

Neal accepted the watch as a symbol of Armstrong's gratitude, even his love. For a number of years, Neal wore it with pride — until the day came that he decided to never put it on his wrist again.

•

Throughout the 1990s, Neal was Armstrong's main soigneur at some domestic races and at national team training camps. But in Europe and at the big races, the honor of rubbing down Armstrong went to John Hendershot.

Among soigneurs in the European peloton (another French word, one that refers to professional riders generally as well as the pack during a race), Hendershot was at once the cool kid and the calculating elder. Other soigneurs envied the money he made and the cachet that came with the cash. Wherever he walked — through race crowds or at home in Belgium — people turned to catch a glimpse. Teams wanted him. Armstrong wanted him. Neal said he was "like a god to me" and called him "the best soigneur that ever was."

Hendershot, an American who lived in Belgium to be closer to the main cycling circuit, was a massage therapist, physical therapist and miracle worker. His laying-on of hands would bring an exhausted, aching rider to life. Eating at Hendershot's direction, sleeping according to his advice, a rider began each morning reborn. He came with all the secrets of a soigneur and an unexpected skill developed over the years. In Neal's words, Hendershot took to cycling's drug culture "like a duck to water." But his enthusiasm for and skills in chemistry would be remembered as his special talent.

Before speaking to me last year, Hendershot — who had retired from the sport in 1996, shortly after Armstrong's cancer diagnosis — had never told his story to a reporter. After all the years of silence, he seemed relieved to finally share it.

For most of a decade, in the 1980s and '90s, Hendershot sat in his makeshift laboratory, preparing for races. There he mixed, matched and mashed up drugs, always with one goal in mind: to make riders go faster. The mad scientist conjured up what he called "weird concoctions" of substances like ephedrine, nicotine, highly concentrated caffeine, drugs that widen blood vessels, blood thinners and testosterone, often trying to find creative ways to give a rider an extra physical boost during a race. He'd pour the mix into tiny bottles and hand them to riders at the starting line. Other times, he'd inject them with it. He wasn't alone in this endeavor. Soigneurs all across Europe made homemade blends of potentially dangerous mixes and first drank or injected those potions into themselves. They were their own lab rats.

Hendershot, who had no formal medical or scientific training, knew a concoction was way off when he felt his heart beating so fast and so loud, it sounded like a runaway freight train. That wouldn't work for riders under extreme physical stress. He wanted "amped up," but not to the point of a heart attack.

It wasn't long before Hendershot tried his potions and pills on the riders, including Armstrong. When Armstrong turned professional after the 1992 Olympics, he signed a contract with Motorola, one of the two major American teams. Because Armstrong wanted the best soigneur, he was immediately paired with Hendershot. It was a match made in doping heaven. Both soigneur and rider were willing to go to the brink of danger.

"What we did was tread the fine line of dropping dead on your bike and winning," Hendershot said.

Hendershot said the riders on his teams had a choice about using drugs. They could "grab the ring or not." He said he didn't know a single professional cyclist who hadn't at least dabbled in doping. The sport was simply too difficult — and many times impossible, as was the three-week Tour de France — for riders who didn't rely on pharmaceutical help.

When Armstrong arrived at Motorola in 1992, a system that facilitated riders' drug use was firmly in place on the team — and most likely in the entire sport. Hendershot said he would take a list of drugs and bogus prescriptions for them to his local pharmacist in Hulste, Belgium, to get them filled and to obtain other drugs, too.

Cycling has been one of Belgium's most popular sports for generations, and the pharmacist didn't question Hendershot's request for such large quantities of drugs. In exchange, Hendershot would give the pharmacist a signed team jersey or all-access passes to big races. Then he would leave with bags filled with the blood booster EPO, human growth hormone, blood thinners, amphetamines, cortisone, painkillers and testosterone, a particularly popular drug he'd hand to riders "like candy."

By 1993, Armstrong was using all of those substances, as did many riders on the team, Hendershot said. He remembered Armstrong's attitude as being, "This is the stuff I take, this is part of what I do," and Armstrong joined the team's program without hesitation because everyone else seemed to be doing it.

"It was like eating team dinner," Hendershot said, adding that he had a hunch that virtually every person knew — doctors, soigneurs, riders, team managers, mechanics. He called the drug use casual and said he never had to hide any of it. After injecting the riders at a team hotel, he'd toss a trash bag filled with syringes and empty vials into the garbage can.

Although Hendershot said he never administered EPO or growth hormone to Armstrong, he did give them to other riders on the team and said he was aware that Armstrong was using those drugs. Hendershot said his wife had driven a stash of those two drugs from Belgium to one of the team's 1995 training camps in southern France.

Riders like Armstrong could get drugs several ways, Hendershot said — from him, from their personal doctors or a doctor who worked with the team, or by buying them over the counter. Each rider would take his drugs to Hendershot, who would administer them by mixing a potion for the rider to drink or inject, or by injecting them into IVs the rider would receive, based on the doctor's instructions. Sometimes, the drugs came in pill form, and Hendershot doled those out, too.

Hendershot was always worried that he was administering something that would hurt the cyclists — or even possibly kill them — especially when they injected the substances into their IVs or when their personal doctors would prepare concoctions for Hendershot to give. He was concerned that he would be culpable if anything ever went wrong. Even as he provided drugs to riders, Hendershot said, he told himself: "You're not a drug dealer. This isn't organized. This is no big deal."

He knew he was lying.

Hendershot rationalized the lie by saying the doping process was overseen by Max Testa, an Italian doctor who is still working in the sport and running a sports medicine clinic in Utah. In 2006, Testa told me that he gave his riders the instructions to use EPO but never administered drugs to those riders. In 2014, he said he didn't want to discuss anything about the cyclists he had worked with, to protect the privacy of his patients. Still, if drug use was not mandated by the team, it appeared to be at least quasi-official. Hendershot trusted Testa to make sure the riders were staying safe, believing that Testa — unlike other doctors in cycling — actually cared for the riders' health, and cared less about winning or money.

Hendershot, however, put it this way: A doctor who refused to give riders drugs wouldn't last in the sport.

Armstrong liked Testa so much that he moved to Italy to be near the doctor's office in Como, north of Milan. Not long after joining Motorola, Armstrong began living in Como during the racing season. He brought along his close friend Frankie Andreu, and in time several other riders joined them, including George Hincapie, a New Yorker, and Kevin Livingston, a Midwesterner. All became patients of Testa. All later became riders on Armstrong's Tour de France-winning United States Postal Service teams.

Hendershot said all those riders probably believed they were doing no wrong by doping. The definition of cheating was flexible in a sport replete with pharmacology: It's not cheating if everybody is doing it.

Armstrong believed that to be the dead-solid truth. For him, there was no hesitation, no second-guessing, no rationalizing.

As Hendershot had done, Armstrong grabbed the ring.

•

It's June 2013, and Armstrong doesn't want to move, he has to. His sponsors have abandoned him, taking away an estimated $75 million in future earnings. He would owe more than $135 million if he lost every lawsuit in which he is a defendant. To "slow the burn rate," as he calls it, he has stopped renting a penthouse near Central Park in Manhattan and a house in Marfa, Tex. Next to go is this Austin estate, traded for a much more modest abode near downtown.

His former sponsors — including Oakley, Trek Bicycle Corporation, RadioShack and Nike — have left him scrambling for money. He considers them traitors. He says Trek's revenue was $100 million when he signed with the company and reached $1 billion in 2013.

"Who's responsible for that?" he asks, before cursing and saying, "Right here." He pokes himself in the chest with his right index finger. "I'm sorry, but that is true. Without me, none of that happens."

After his sponsors cast him aside, he tossed their gear. There's a chance you could catch a glimpse of one of his Dallas friends wearing Armstrong's custom-made yellow Nike sneakers, with "Lance" embroidered in small yellow block letters on the black tongues. A Goodwill outlet in Austin is supplied with his Nike clothes and Oakley sunglasses. The movers will have to contend with whatever brand-name gear is left in his garage: black Livestrong Nike caps, black Nike duffel bags with bright yellow swooshes, Oakley lenses and frames and a box of caps suggesting "Yes on Prop 15," a 2007 Texas bond plan for cancer research, prevention and education supported by Armstrong.

Armstrong loves this house. He loves its open spaces and floor-to-ceiling windows. He loves the lush landscaped yard where his children play soccer, and the crystalline pool (a "negative-edge pool, not an infinity pool, get it right," he said). Behind the house are rows of towering Italian cypresses.

He moved here in 2006 after winning a record seventh Tour de France. He once said the place was his safe house — inside it, "nobody's going to mess with me." Having eluded continual attempts to expose his doping, he could take a left down the main hallway, then a quick right, and disappear into his walk-in wine closet to grab a bottle of Tignanello and toast his good luck.

Seven years ago, he told his three children from his failed marriage — Luke, Grace and Isabelle — that they would graduate from high school while living in the house by the big oak tree. He owed them that. They had followed him from Texas to France to Spain countless times. At last they could plant some roots. "I promise," he said. "Dad's not moving again."

But now the movers are coming. It's June 6, 2013, five years before Luke's expected graduation. The next morning, a line of black trucks will pull into his driveway and out will spill workers in black short-sleeve shirts. The atmosphere is funereal. A week earlier, the movers emptied the 1,633-square-foot guesthouse, a minimansion, with its matching tan facade and burnt orange roof.

I return the next day to see those workers clear the main house. They take Armstrong's Tour trophies from their illuminated shelves, cover them with green bubble wrap and place them in blue boxes. In a box marked #64, one mover places a silver frame containing a 5x7 photograph of Armstrong's 2005 Discovery Channel team sitting at a dinner table after his seventh and final Tour victory. He, his teammates and his longtime team manager Johan Bruyneel are holding up seven fingers. A yellow rubber Livestrong bracelet hangs from each man's wrist. A table is littered with half-empty wineglasses. A former life.

Box 64 goes onto the truck with the rest. I follow the movers into the media room. Wearing white cotton gloves, they take down the seven yellow Tour leader's jerseys framed above the couch.

In the dark before dawn, Armstrong left the big house for good.

At 4:15 a.m. on June 7, 2013, with his girlfriend, Anna Hansen, and his five children, he drove to Austin-Bergstrom International Airport for a commercial flight to Hawaii, where they would remain for the first part of the summer.

Armstrong tells me he didn't look back at the house he had built. He says sentiment has never been his thing. The move means only that part of his life has ended and another will begin. That's all it is, he says.

Several days later, only two of his possessions remained on his estate. One couldn't fit in the moving truck: a 1970 black Pontiac GTO convertible given him by the singer Sheryl Crow, with whom he had a very public romance that ended when he pedaled away just before she got cancer. The car, with its evocations of another Armstrong failure, carries a price tag of $70,000.

And, finally, left over in the living room of the guesthouse was a fully assembled drum kit. Just another piece of the man's discarded life. Oh beat the drum slowly and play the fife lowly, I thought while I looked at the set, lyrics from "Streets of Laredo," a song I know from my time working in Texas.

Take me to the valley, and lay the sod o'er me,
For I'm a young cowboy and I know I've done wrong.

This article comprises excerpts from "Cycle of Lies: The Fall of Lance Armstrong," by Juliet Macur, a sports columnist for The New York Times.

Exchanging Sword for Pen, Rodriguez Apologizes to Yankees and Fans

BY DAVID WALDSTEIN | FEB. 17, 2015

TAMPA, FLA. — Preparing to make a highly scrutinized return to baseball after a long suspension for drug use, Alex Rodriguez issued a brief, handwritten statement on Tuesday afternoon to say he was sorry for his behavior.

It was Rodriguez's first public comment on the matter since he issued a defiant statement in January 2014, the day his suspension went into effect. Back then, he said the charges against him were false. Thirteen months later, writing in cursive in an apparent attempt to add a personal touch, Rodriguez demonstrated some contrition.

BARTON SILVERMAN/THE NEW YORK TIMES

New York Yankees shortstop Alex Rodriguez at Yankee Stadium in 2013.

While not directly admitting to the use of performance-enhancing drugs, the matter at the heart of his suspension, he tacitly acknowledged that the record 162-game penalty against him had been warranted and said that the misdeeds had been his own.

"To the fans," his statement began. "I take full responsibility for the mistakes that led to my suspension for the 2014 season. I regret that my actions made the situation worse than it needed to be. To Major League Baseball, the Yankees, the Steinbrenner family, the players association and you, the fans, I can only say I'm sorry.

"I accept the fact that many of you will not believe my apology or anything that I say at this point," the statement added. "I understand why, and that's on me."

The timing of the statement coincided with the release of an article in ESPN the Magazine. In it, Rodriguez suggested that in recent seasons he had actually been given placebos, and not performance enhancers, by Anthony Bosch, the former head of the Biogenesis clinic in Miami. On Tuesday, Bosch was sentenced to four years in prison for his activities with Biogenesis.

"Only a dope like me would do that stuff and have the two worst statistical seasons of my career," Rodriguez said in the article.

Rodriguez was not the only major leaguer who turned to Bosch, and his now-defunct clinic, to gain access to banned substances. Twelve other major leaguers did so as well, and were also suspended by baseball, but not with the severity to which Rodriguez was subjected. And only Rodriguez attempted to get out of his punishment.

It is unclear what Rodriguez has planned for the next stage of his return, and whether it will include a formal news conference before his anticipated arrival here next week for the start of spring training. It also remains to be seen what questions he might be willing to answer when he does finally engage in some sort of face-to-face session with the news media.

The Yankees have forbidden him to use their spring training complex to hold a formal news conference, mindful, perhaps, of the uproar he created there in 2009, when he admitted, to an assembled throng of reporters, that he had used steroids earlier in his career.

This time, the Yankees concluded, it would better for that scene to play out in the Bronx, at Yankee Stadium. The Yankees told Rodriguez that that was their preference, but Rodriguez has now ruled out that option, saying in his statement that it was "gracious" for the Yankees to suggest he go the Bronx but that he was not going to take them up on the offer.

"I decided the next time I am in Yankee Stadium, I should be in pinstripes doing my job," the statement said.

So where will Rodriguez answer whatever questions he is willing to answer? If he decides on an informal setting, he could simply do it at his locker in the Tampa clubhouse, though that would certainly disrupt the Yankees' routine.

For that reason, team executives were not particularly pleased with Tuesday's developments. They were hoping an extensive news conference by Rodriguez, away from Tampa, might shift the focus back to baseball. Now they are not sure what comes next.

The statement on Tuesday echoed similar apologies Rodriguez had already made to Major League Baseball, the Yankees and the players association earlier this month, not only for using drugs provided by Bosch but also for the combative and litigious approach he took while initially trying to avoid a suspension.

"I served the longest suspension in the history of the League for PED use," Rodriguez said at one point in the statement. "The commissioner has said the matter is over. The players association has said the same. The Yankees have said the next step is to play baseball. I'm ready to put this chapter behind me and play some ball.

"This game has been my single biggest passion since I was a teenager," Rodriguez added. "When I go to spring training, I will do everything I can to be the best player and teammate possible, earn a spot on the Yankees and help us win."

Rodriguez signed the statement, "Sincerely, Alex."

For the last several months, Rodriguez has kept a low profile while working out in Miami and Los Angeles. But in the hours following the arbitrator's adverse ruling on his suspension, on Jan. 11, 2014, Rodriguez was breathing fire. He issued a statement that day saying, in part: "I have been clear that I did not use performance-enhancing substances as alleged in the notice of discipline, or violate the Basic Agreement or the Joint Drug Agreement in any manner, and in order to prove it I will take this fight to Federal Court."

He added at the time, "No player should have to go through what I have been dealing with, and I am exhausting all options."

And yet by the end of that month, Rodriguez had admitted to federal prosecutors in the Biogenesis case that he had indeed used Bosch to provide him with performance enhancers. By that point, he had also decided to drop any effort to challenge the arbitrator's ruling in the courts. From there, he proceeded to serve out his season-long suspension and, more recently, begin his series of apologies.

Tuesday's statement, and apology, came six years to the day after Rodriguez held a news conference at the Yankees' facility in Tampa to acknowledge that he had used a cousin to help him obtain and use steroids during a period between 2001 and 2003, when he was playing for the Texas Rangers.

At the time, Rodriguez explained his behavior as being the "silly and irresponsible" actions of a "young guy."

Now he is old, at least by baseball standards. He turns 40 in July and will attempt to play this season with two surgically repaired hips after missing all of the 2014 campaign and much of 2013 as well, when he was rehabilitating from his second operation.

Recognizing all that, the Yankees are not counting on him for much this season except the inevitable distractions. During the winter, they signed Chase Headley, a third baseman, to a four-year extension, leaving Rodriguez without a position, except that of designated hitter, assuming he even hits enough to justify a spot in the lineup.

Nevertheless, Rodriguez still has three years and $61 million guaranteed remaining on his enormous contract, plus extra marketing clauses that theoretically could earn him an additional $6 million apiece in bonuses if he can reach various milestones on the career home run list.

The first of those milestones is Willie Mays's total of 660 home runs. Rodriguez, with 654, is just six away. The Yankees have informed Rodriguez they do not intend to honor the bonus payments because they were part of a separate marketing agreement that was not part of his 10-year contract and that, as a drug violator, he is no longer marketable.

Whether the Yankees' stance will be upheld if Rodriguez challenges it is in question. Whether Rodriguez will ever get to 660 is not a certainty, either. The only thing for sure at the moment is that the long-running Rodriguez saga is back in full bloom.

The Home Run Explosion Is Not Exactly Beyond Suspicion

BY MICHAEL POWELL | SEPT. 21, 2017

THE RECORD-SETTING 5,694th home run of the 2017 season soared over the right-center-field fence in Toronto earlier this week. And the talk afterward among coaches and players centered on launch angles and physics and miraculous epiphanies about the virtue of pulling the baseball.

Haven't we seen this show before?

I wandered the nation writing on national politics in 1998, and each night I tuned in to watch Sammy Sosa and Mark McGwire wallop balls into the farthest reaches of St. Louis and Wrigley. Oh, baby, those balls never came down.

McGwire and Sosa had big bats and biceps that would have made Popeye blush, and they obliterated the single-season home run record. Please, no questions about chemical helpers. This was physics. Greatness was happening.

It was a steroidal farce.

I appreciate that baseball players and officials have taken big strides to clean up doping in their sport. And I dig transcendent achievement in athletics. But my every reflex argues against too quickly taking this home run explosion at face value.

Baseball writers whom I much respect offer learned exegeses on revolutionary batting techniques and the physics of hitting a baseball. A wonky subset has concentrated on the baseball itself, speculating that it is souped up. The theorists in this group bounce the ball, cut it open and rub their hands over the seams like members of a cargo cult.

Most nod to the possibility of steroids, if only to wave it off as improbable. Testing and tough penalties, they say, argue against a revival.

O.K., maybe, but not really.

Such arguments require that we ignore lived memory, not to mention experience gleaned from other sports. Track, cycling, tennis, swimming, the biathlon and downhill skiing: These sports have antidoping regimens even tougher than baseball's — a track athlete can face a four-year ban for a first offense — and have made genuine strides.

Yet a determined subset of athletes in these sports get their hands on performance-enhancing drugs and evade testing regimens. Are we to believe that a major league second baseman will opt to remain a teetotaler if 10 more home runs could turn him into an $18-million-per-year star?

I called an investigator with wide experience in the world of doping. "Am I being unfair to ask?" I began. His laughter cut me off. There are testosterone creams, he said, that disappear without a trace. There are drugs like growth factor 1 for which there are no reliable tests.

This is not to deny a march of reform. In the 1990s, the Lords of Baseball could not have been more complicit in the steroid era had Commissioner Bud Selig kept a bottle of Stanozolol on his desk. That changed. Baseball players and owners embraced reform. Testing procedures began and then grew tougher, and the players union eventually agreed to add blood testing, which is needed to find evidence of human growth hormone.

The players and owners deserve applause.

Yet let me play skunk at the garden party. Baseball catches just a handful of reprobates each year. And most are using Brezhnev-era steroids. A Mets relief pitcher, Jenrry Mejia, pulled off a bonehead trifecta last year, being nabbed for the third time in 18 months for use of a crude anabolic steroid.

Baseball also catches a tiny handful of players using more sophisticated drugs, including peptides and H.G.H. The biggest haul of players nabbed for using more advanced drugs came in the Biogenesis scandal of 2013, which netted more than a dozen players, including the bionic Alex Rodriguez.

For the most part, they were tripped up by paper evidence, not drug tests. Are we to assume that baseball players, faced with the possibility of absurd riches, now refuse to delve into this modern world of drugs?

I'll put no names to suspicions. Many baseball players perform clean and deserve not to get a raised eyebrow from the likes of me. Players have career years, along with chiropractors who unlock their hips. Sometimes their launch angles really are NASA-ready.

But this explosion of home runs is suspicion-inducing. In ancient times, which is to say the 2014 season, 11 players hit 30 or more home runs. This season, 32 players are projected to clear the 30-home run mark. In 2014, a scrappy bunch of Kansas City Royals battled into the World Series. They had just three players who broke into double figures with home runs.

This year, the Royals are a less formidable team, and they have four players with at least 20 home runs; the team leader has already hit 37. Eight Yankees have hit more than 10 home runs, and two have smacked more than 30. The broken-down Mets have 10 players in double figures this year.

Many point to physics, as though baseball were suddenly thick with budding Albert Einsteins. Batters and coaches have discovered launch angles, which is to say the upper cut, and concentrate on pulling the ball. As if it never occurred to earlier generations of stars — Willie Mays, Henry Aaron, Ted Williams and Willie Stargell — to take an upper cut? As for pulling the ball, McCovey Cove in San Francisco is so named because Willie McCovey, that old long-ball hitter, poled home run after home run straight down the line and over right-field fences.

Let me indulge my inner wonk. I took a dozen of this year's top home run hitters and went to Fangraphs.com and checked spray charts, which show where their home runs landed. If players have begun pulling the ball relentlessly, we might expect to see a dramatic increase in home runs hit to their power side.

Yet most had hit the same percentage of home runs to different corners of stadiums as in years past. They have simply hit more of them.

Some speculate that coaches and pitchers have become enraptured with the fastball and that big men now throw too many of the 98 m.p.h. variety. When batters connect, that ball travels a long way.

Alas, in 2014 writers and coaches relied on this same phenomenon to help explain why batters hit so few home runs that year. Sports Illustrated headlined a 2014 story "The Case of the Disappearing Slugger." It speculated that we would see many more hitters returning to batting styles that put an emphasis on smarts and using all fields.

A year earlier Bleacher Report had argued the home run drought was proof that the door had closed on the steroid era.

Arguably, baseball's current state is consistent with doping's history, which is to say athletes become more careful after their peers are caught.

Track offers a good example. The 1980s and 1990s were the Wild West era of doping, and records fell with startling regularity. A crackdown followed, stars were caught and banned, and questionable records remained in place for years.

The men's 400-meter record held up for 16 years until it was broken last year. More startling, Marita Koch, an East German woman whose nation engaged in state-run doping, has held the women's record in the 400-meter run since 1985.

In other words, athletes who chose to dope and their handlers carefully seek out that narrow band between chemical advantage and exposure. And the results are less noticeable.

It is at least plausible baseball has traveled this route. The early users shot and ingested, and records fell. Then the sport's greatest stars began to use, and like Icarus, they flew too close to the sun. Barry Bonds, who was directly linked to a doping scandal, slammed 73 home runs in 2001, breaking McGwire's record from 1998.

That ostentatious display arguably led to the exposure of the steroid era. If players are using now, they are likely to be doing so more discreetly.

I confess I'm no fan of these home run effusions, whether driven by steroid or technique. It's a dullard's game, strikeouts, power and little else. If we're to live in this era of massive power, however, let's at least seek an honest reckoning.

Lance Armstrong Settles Federal Fraud Case for $5 Million

BY JULIET MACUR | APRIL 19, 2018

LANCE ARMSTRONG AGREED on Thursday to pay $5 million to settle claims that he defrauded the federal government by using performance-enhancing drugs when the United States Postal Service sponsored his cycling team.

The settlement ended years of legal wrangling between Armstrong and the government over whether the Postal Service had actually sustained harm because of Armstrong's doping.

After years of vehement denials, Armstrong admitted in 2013 that he had used banned substances while winning a record seven Tour de France titles from 1999 to 2005. He wore a Postal Service jersey during the first six of those victories, but he was stripped of all his Tour titles in 2012 after an investigation by the United States Anti-Doping Agency determined that he and many of his teammates had been doping.

"We've had exactly the same view of this case forever, which was that it was a bogus case because the Postal Service was never harmed," Elliot Peters, Armstrong's lead lawyer, said in a telephone interview.

He added that the Postal Service had boasted that sponsoring Armstrong's cycling team for $32.3 million was a marketing boon. That was the value of the second deal between the Postal Service and the team. That contract, unlike its predecessor, contained an antidoping clause.

If he had lost in court, Armstrong faced the possibility of paying treble damages under the terms of the False Claims Act, which is aimed at recovering government money obtained by fraud. The government could have demanded nearly $100 million.

The settlement averted a trial scheduled to begin with jury selection in about two weeks in Federal District Court in Washington.

“I am particularly glad to have made peace with the Postal Service,” Armstrong said in a statement issued by Peters’s law firm. “While I believe that their lawsuit against me was without merit and unfair, I have since 2013 tried to take full responsibility for my mistakes, and make amends wherever possible. I rode my heart out for the Postal cycling team, and was always especially proud to wear the red, white and blue eagle on my chest when competing in the Tour de France. Those memories are very real and mean a lot to me.”

The prospect of losing his fortune had loomed over Armstrong, 46, since the case was filed in 2010. It was the most daunting of the legal woes that have dogged him since he confessed. A statement from Peters’s law firm said the settlement had ended “all litigation against Armstrong related to his 2013 admission that during his career as a professional cyclist he had used performance-enhancing substances.”

Floyd Landis, a former teammate of Armstrong’s, was the original plaintiff in the case, acting as a whistle-blower with a chance to receive a share of any money recovered by the government.

The government chose to join the case after Armstrong’s confession in 2013, and the Postal Service claimed it would not have sponsored the team if it had known Armstrong was doping.

Landis, who also doped during his cycling career and was stripped of the 2006 Tour de France title, will receive $1.1 million of the government’s $5 million. In addition to the $5 million settlement, Armstrong will pay $1.65 million to cover Landis’s legal costs, according to lawyers for both Landis and Armstrong.

“It has been a difficult ordeal, and public opinion was not always on my side,” Landis said in a statement from his lawyer’s office. “But it was the right thing to do and I am hopeful that some positive changes for cycling and sport in general will be the result.”

The government considered pursuing criminal fraud charges against Armstrong almost a year before he confessed, but it dropped the case.

"No one is above the law," Chad A. Readler, the acting assistant attorney general for the Justice Department's civil division, said Thursday in a statement. "A competitor who intentionally uses illegal P.E.D.s not only deceives fellow competitors and fans, but also sponsors, who help make sporting competitions possible. This settlement demonstrates that those who cheat the government will be held accountable."

Soccer and Doping? Don't Ask, Don't Tell

OPINION | BY MUSA OKWONGA | JUNE 26, 2018

THE WORLD CUP continues to thrill, with exhilarating wins by England, Germany, Belgium and Colombia, and an equally exciting draw between Japan and Senegal. Away from the field, though, an old controversy has once again rumbled into view: doping.

The Mail on Sunday, a British newspaper, reported over the weekend that a Russian player, Ruslan Kambolov, who was excluded from his country's World Cup squad because of injury, had tested positive for performance-enhancing drugs 18 months ago. And according to the paper, it gets worse: Both the Russian authorities and FIFA kept this information quiet.

FIFA has swiftly rejected this version of events, stating that "insufficient evidence was found to assert an antidoping rule violation by any footballer." But in some ways, it doesn't matter. Even before FIFA's denial, the story attracted little scandal. Among football fans these days, reports of doping are generally met with a shrug.

Why? Well, for one thing, drug use isn't new to football. In a 2013 interview, Johnny Rep, who starred for Ajax and Holland in the 1970s, said that it was common to take amphetamines before matches. More recently, there were allegations that Spanish players had enhanced their performance by receiving artificially oxygenated blood. FIFA itself has expelled players from the World Cup for drug use: Willie Johnston of Scotland in 1978 and most infamously Argentina's Diego Maradona in 1994.

Given all of that, and the steady stream of doping stories across professional sports in recent years, many fans may at this point have anger fatigue. On some level, maybe we've just accepted that drug use is an inevitable part of elite sports.

It's not hard to reach this conclusion. Football, for one, is astonishingly competitive, and it's getting faster all the time. The margins for success are getting smaller and smaller. As Amit Katwala has noted, "In 2006, when Germany finished third in the World Cup, their players spent an average of 2.9 seconds on the ball each time they had it. By 2014, when they won, that had fallen to just 0.9 seconds." In other words, footballers at the highest level now have much less time to pass the ball before they are tackled.

What's more, the sheer number of games that teams must play means that there is an extraordinary toll taken on players' endurance. Each infinitesimal advantage counts, and unfathomable amounts of money and prestige are at stake. It's hardly surprising that the pressure to seek illegal advantage, through artificially increasing stamina, may at times feel overwhelming.

And yet it sometimes seems that football and its fans have a "Don't ask, don't tell" policy in place when it comes to doping. Like the consumers of delicious fast-food chicken nuggets, we may be less than comfortable knowing how our meal has been produced.

There may come a time when authorities take a more pragmatic view, assume that doping has become an inescapable part of the game, and seek not to outlaw it but to regulate it. Until then, though, it looks as if we may have to maintain the veil of innocence around the beautiful game, even as it continues to unravel.

On that happy thought, I've got to go get ready to watch a match! Last week, I wrote about how much I wanted to see an African team succeed in the World Cup, given the continent's history. Since then, Senegal has impressed me a lot. And this afternoon, Nigeria, which has had a stirring resurgence in recent days, faces off against Argentina — and its last chance to advance to the next round. I'll be keeping my fingers crossed.

MUSA OKWONGA is a poet and writer based in Berlin. He is the author of two books on football, "A Cultured Left Foot" and "Will You Manage?"

CHAPTER 5

Falling Through the Cracks

When sports stars are accused of doping, their first response is usually angry denunciations, but often the evidence proves them wrong. Sometimes, though, an element of doubt exists, as with the doping of Iditarod dogs in late 2017. Doping tests are not infallible, either. Some do not take into account athletes' unique body chemistry. Others seem to be administered unfairly. Doping substances like caffeine have different effects based on genes. The role of testosterone in women is an ongoing issue with testing, too.

Dog Doping at the Iditarod: Dallas Seavey, a Legend in the Sport, Is Named

BY BENJAMIN HOFFMAN | OCT. 23, 2017

IN A MAJOR BLOW to the integrity of the Iditarod dog-sled race, officials for the sport on Monday identified the four-time champion Dallas Seavey as the musher whose dogs recently tested positive for banned drugs in this year's competition.

Seavey, whose family is full-fledged Iditarod royalty, had his string of three consecutive victories in the annual race, which runs through the Alaskan wilderness, broken in March by his father, Mitch. Father beat son by a little less than three hours and in the process broke Dallas Seavey's world record, which had been set in 2016.

Earlier this month, the Iditarod Trail Committee made the surprising announcement that four of the dogs in this year's event had tested positive for the opioid pain reliever Tramadol. It was the first time dogs had tested positive for a prohibited substance since the race began testing in 1994.

Despite the positive test, the committee said Seavey would be allowed to participate in next year's race and would not face any discipline because of what it called an "ambiguous rule" that requires them to establish the musher's intent. But in a Facebook post, Seavey linked to a lengthy statement he made in a YouTube video and said he had withdrawn his name from the 2018 competition in protest.

"The Iditarod can try to run me over, they can try to throw me under the bus," Seavey said in the video, "but I'm going to be honest to myself and they're going to find out that I don't fit under the bus."

As a result of the violation, race officials said, they reworked the rules to establish clearer standards for what constitutes a violation and for how a musher's culpability can be proved or disproved. The revision to the regulation, known as Rule 39, stipulates penalties for violations, including disqualification or even a ban from future competition.

According to the committee's statement that identified Seavey, he denied that he had administered the drug and said that doing so would have been irrational since he was aware of the testing. He said that Tramadol, in his opinion, would not give him a competitive advantage, according to the statement.

But in his video, Seavey went further, calling the proceedings "a cancer" on the sport and saying he believes the positive test was the result of a malicious attack from either another musher or from one of the protest groups that wants to harm the Iditarod. He said he was told in April about the positive result and had tried to work with the board to make the information public in order to exonerate himself but that the board would not work with him. He also said he expected ramifications for speaking up.

ANCHORAGE DAILY NEWS/TRIBUNE NEWS SERVICE/GETTY IMAGES

Dallas Seavey gets a kiss from one of his dogs after crossing under the burled arch in Nome, Alaska, to win the 2014 Iditarod Trail Sled Dog Race on Tuesday, March 11, 2014.

"I fully expect that after this I will be banned from the Iditarod based on the gag rule," he said, making reference to a rule he claimed prevents mushers from discussing internal matters.

The committee initially kept Seavey's identity secret, but after an emergency session on Monday they reversed course and named him because of a "level of unhealthy speculation involved in this matter."

The pressure had come largely from the Iditarod Official Finishers Club, which issued a statement signed by 83 current and former competitors demanding the identity of the musher in question be revealed.

"It is unacceptable that multiple dogs tested positive for a drug in a single musher's team and that that information was only recently made public when it was known since shortly after the team finished," the statement said.

That it was a member of the Seavey family adds a great deal of weight to the issue, considering their importance to the race's history. Dallas Seavey, 30, was the youngest musher to win the Iditarod when he captured the 2012 title, and he also won in 2014, 2015 and 2016. His father has three titles, as well as the world record time. His wife, Jen, ran the race in 2009, and his grandfather, Dan, competed in the first two Iditarod races in 1973 and 1974.

After his fourth Iditarod win, Dallas Seavey explained what the accomplishment meant to his family, saying "It's just another day of mushing, man. This is what we do."

Iditarod Doping Mystery: Who Slipped Tramadol to the Dogs?

BY JOHN BRANCH | OCT. 24, 2017

JUST WHEN THE SPORTS WORLD thought it had heard it all in doping — someone spiked my toothpaste, a masseur rubbed me with tainted ointment, those unexplained stem cells in my blood came, of course, from my unborn twin in utero — along comes the Iditarod.

A doping scandal has hit the world's most famous dog-sled race, the 1,000-mile trek through Alaska that ends in Nome each March. Four dogs on a team run by Dallas Seavey, a four-time champion and the most dominant musher in the sport, tested positive last spring for high levels of Tramadol, an opioid pain reliever.

Seavey finished second at this year's Iditarod behind his father, Mitch, who ended his son's three-year winning streak. The younger Seavey was identified as the doping dogs' musher on Monday, lifting the sport into headlines and punch lines.

There is no proof that Seavey was the one who gave his dogs the drug, and he sternly claimed his innocence in a nearly 18-minute soliloquy posted to YouTube on Monday. He suggested a likely, if familiar, explanation: sabotage.

"Sabotage is a likely case," Seavey said. "If it was not another musher — and believe me, I hope it was not — there are many other people that could do the same thing."

It was a familiar response in the sports world. When confronted with allegations of doping, deny. When pressed, raise a possible explanation, no matter how outlandish it sounds. The sprinter Justin Gatlin and the baseball slugger Barry Bonds tried to pin accusations on a rubbed-in ointment. The middle-distance runner Dieter Baumann blamed spiked toothpaste. The cyclist Tyler Hamilton forwarded the vanishing-twin theory, suggesting that the blood in his body that wasn't his own could be explained by a twin he had that died in utero.

Like most excuses, they were mocked and later deemed invalid.

One thing that makes this case different — besides the athletes in question being dogs, not humans — is that many of Seavey's competitors believe his excuse. Several top mushers defended him and echoed his theory that something unknown and untoward was at play in the backwoods of Alaska.

"I don't believe for a second he did it — not for one second," said Jessie Royer, who finished fifth at the Iditarod. "He's not that way. He's an honest, hardworking person, and he sure as hell isn't dumb enough to give dogs Tramadol hours before a drug test."

But if Seavey did not give his dogs the banned substance, who did? Was it a jealous competitor? An anti-dogsledding activist looking to undermine the sport's top race and top racer?

Those questions percolated across the mushing community on Tuesday, leaving many perplexed. Aliy Zirkle, who finished eighth this year and has raced against Seavey for a decade, called him "an honest and upstanding Iditarod competitor," not the type to break rules.

"I do not think that he gave those drugs to his dogs," Zirkle said in an email. "Obviously his dogs were given drugs — but by whom or why? I don't know."

The thought that another musher would taint Seavey's dogs sounded unlikely to his competitors. The sport is a tight and insular one, in constant need of sponsors and promotion, and setting off a doping scandal would hurt the sport as much as it would damage Seavey. And Tramadol would be a strange drug choice; it is not commonly used in the world of dogsledding. Royer said she had never heard of it.

That reasoning led some to speculate that outsiders who protest the Iditarod and similar events might be involved.

"There are people in the world who truly believe that dog mushing is cruel and should be banned," Zirkle said. "Of course, this is far from the truth, but lies can be told about any subject and some people believe them. I guess the question is: Are there really people radical enough to actually give drugs to his dogs in order to undermine an honest, hardworking good man? Crazy speculation, I know! But that seems to be all we are left with now."

Unless, of course, Seavey did it. The Iditarod Trail Committee, which stages the event, does not seem convinced. It did not discipline Seavey, nor ask him to return the $59,637 he won in prize money, because it could not prove intent, as was required by race rules. After the positive tests emerged, the first ones since the race began drug testing the dogs in 1994, the group examined rules in other sports and realized it was virtually alone in not placing the burden of proof on the athlete — in this case, the musher, not the dogs. It changed the rule earlier this month and, in announcing those changes, brought Seavey's drug-test results to light.

"If you look at the intent, why would a musher want to do something like that so close to the finish line?" an Iditarod spokesman, Chas St. George, said. "That musher knows that he or she is going to be subject to a test. It's speculative, it's not evidentiary, but you have to ask that question."

The closest parallel to the Iditarod case may be an episode at the 1968 Kentucky Derby, won by Dancer's Image, who tested positive for the painkiller Phenylbutazone. The horse's owner, Peter D. Fuller, futilely suggested that someone had sneaked into the horse's stall and administered the drug. Dancer's Image remains the only winning horse to be disqualified from the Derby.

These days, top horse races have guidelines about security and surveillance of the horses, sometimes with 24-hour cameras in the stalls.

The Iditarod is different. When it comes to drug testing and consistent monitoring of the dogs, the event is rife with logistical challenges that may be unique in sports — a 1,000-mile race through the wilderness that lasted more than eight days for this year's top teams, each of which started with 16 dogs (usually Alaskan huskies).

Typically, officials conduct urine tests at the ceremonial start in Anchorage, at the finish line in Nome, and randomly at the roughly three-dozen checkpoints along the way.

At the start and finish, and in larger towns along the way, fans often get close to the dogs.

"We invite spectators to pet our dogs, we share intimate stories about mushing and we hope that people celebrate dog mushing and our huskies like we do," Zirkle said. "It is for this reason it would not be difficult to have walked up to any one of Dallas's dogs after the race or even during the event and given them a drugged biscuit or treat. His dogs, like mine, are incredibly friendly and are used to kind gestures and treats."

Mushers are usually nearby, as are veterinarians and volunteer race officials, but not always. At checkpoints, mushers usually feed the dogs, massage them, try to get them to rest, and restock the sled with supplies. Sometimes they will leave the dogs alone while they go into a tent to nap or eat.

"You have to remember how remote this race is," Royer said. "If someone really wanted to do something, I guess they could. Usually that's not a concern, at least not in the past."

A major area of concern, at least now, are the food drops that teams have shipped to places along the course. The Iditarod drops up to 90 tons of the shipments, usually a few weeks before the race begins. Seavey said they could easily be sabotaged. St. George said the Iditarod was looking into ways to ensure the food drops would not be tampered with, perhaps through more security and surveillance.

Creating foolproof security around dozens of checkpoints, hundreds of dogs and a thousand miles of a remote course is a daunting task. Royer half-joked that someone could probably leave laced meatballs on the course and dogs might scoop them up.

One other thing makes the Iditarod case different than others in sports: It is likely to go unsolved. Without a full investigation — where to start, and who will do it? — there probably is no way to know for sure what happened to Seavey's dogs.

"That's the tough part, actually," St. George said. "Having closure on something like this would be the most preferred outcome. But we don't."

Critics Say FIFA Is Stalling a Doping Inquiry as World Cup Nears

BY TARIQ PANJA | JAN. 3, 2018

LONDON — Dealing with sports Russia and its doping program haunted the International Olympic Committee for over a year. Now it's FIFA's turn.

With the Russia World Cup six months away, leaders of the antidoping movement are criticizing soccer's governing body over its failure to pursue more aggressively whether Russian authorities covered up positive doping tests belonging to the country's top soccer players.

Travis Tygart, the head of the United States Anti-Doping Agency, said Tuesday that FIFA's apparent inaction was "exasperating." Craig Reedie, the president of the World Anti-Doping Agency, said he expected FIFA to pursue any allegations of corruption and act decisively.

"We provided them with all the information we had at the time and told them they should be responsible for getting on with results management," Reedie said.

At issue is whether FIFA has made every effort to contact Grigory Rodchenkov, the Russian whistle-blower and former director of the Moscow laboratory for drug testing whose testimony unmasked a vast doping program that corrupted global sports across several Olympics, with evidence extending from 2011 to 2015.

FIFA said it initially tried to contact Rodchenkov last year through WADA but was told he was not available. In a statement Tuesday, FIFA said it was awaiting the reanalysis of the samples of Russian athletes who were implicated by a trove of data obtained from Moscow in November before trying to re-establish contact with Rodchenkov. The reanalysis of the doping samples, expected to happen later this month, may be necessary to establish further evidence to successfully discipline athletes. The lab in Switzerland that is conducting the analysis is giving priority to samples from the tainted 2014 Winter Olympics before the Winter Games next month in South Korea.

"FIFA will continue its investigations, working in close collaboration with WADA and exploring every possible avenue," FIFA officials said in the prepared statement.

James Walden, a lawyer for Rodchenkov, said FIFA officials had never gotten in touch with him.

Tygart said that was unacceptable. "Frankly, it's exasperating. Clean athletes and the public deserve to have the impact of Russian doping on football, if any, resolved immediately. We are over three years into dealing with this mess and there is no excuse for FIFA failing to contact the star witness at this point," Tygart said Tuesday.

Rodchenkov is currently in hiding in the United States. His testimony ultimately led to the International Olympic Committee's decision in December to ban Russia's Olympic Committee from next month's Winter Olympics. After conducting their own investigation, the I.O.C.'s investigators surmised that Rodchenkov, branded a traitor in Russia, had largely been telling the truth.

Rodchenkov has evidence of Russian soccer players being protected by the state doping program, according to Walden. Those claims first appeared in the explosive 2016 report for the World Anti-Doping Agency from the Canadian lawyer Richard McLaren. McLaren based his report on forensic evidence and the cooperation of Rodchenkov. The report said more than 1,000 athletes from across 30 sports may have had their samples covered up, including soccer players that were on Russia's 2014 World Cup roster.

FIFA released a timeline of its investigation so far, which has yielded no evidence of doping by Russian soccer players. Critics say the organization is trying to avoid acrimony with the country that is playing host to the World Cup next summer. FIFA said if it can find evidence "to demonstrate an antidoping rule violation by any athlete, FIFA will impose the appropriate sanction."

"For all the time and work FIFA put into this defensive timeline, it could have picked up the phone and arranged an interview of Dr. Rodchenkov 10 times over," said Walden, the lawyer for Rodchenkov.

Rodchenkov remains an active participant in the ongoing process in which scores of athletes have been barred following a reanalysis of their samples. He plans to provide witness testimony to the Court of Arbitration for Sport during appeals proceedings for sanctioned Russian athletes.

FIFA is trying to manage the doping inquiry amid lingering scrutiny of its ability to reform in the aftermath of a sprawling corruption scandal in 2015. That scandal brought down most of its top leadership. Three of its former governance leaders recently published an article in which they concluded FIFA couldn't be trusted to change under its own steam, and that outside intervention was needed.

Tygart said FIFA's performance showed "why reform to the global antidoping system must start with removing sport from attempting to police itself, because you can't both promote and police effectively — as this clearly shows."

The Russia World Cup has had other problems, too. Sponsors have been slow to sign on for what is the world's most-watched event. Russia's broadcasters finally signed a deal to broadcast the tournament in late December after more than a year of balking at FIFA's demands.

President Gianni Infantino's efforts to generate excitement for the tournament were torpedoed when a news conference before last month's World Cup draw was overshadowed by questions about doping and the continued presence of Vitaly Mutko, Russia's deputy prime minister, as head of the organizing committee. Mutko had days earlier received a lifetime ban from the Olympics for his role in the doping scandal. He had been Russia's sports minister at the time of the Sochi Games.

Mutko has since stepped down from the organizing committee and temporarily resigned from his post as head of Russian soccer's governing body.

Jiri Dvorak, FIFA's top doctor for 22 years until his ouster in October 2016, expressed surprise that his former employers had yet to reach out to Rodchenkov. Dvorak had an active role the last time a drugs scandal threatened to overcome the tournament.

In 1994, he resisted pressure from some of FIFA's most senior officials when the Argentine superstar Diego Maradona, then among the most famous men on the planet, was ousted for failing a drug test. "That was against opinion of some of the South Americans. But Maradona had to be removed because when it comes to things like this you have to act according to the laws and the regulations," he said.

The I.O.C. has defended its own prolonged investigation that ultimately reiterated what had largely been known for more than a year. The organization blamed the delay on the challenge of coming up with a scientific test that could categorically confirm the claims that bottles containing urine samples had been tampered with. Investigators in November also secured the crucial data from Russia's drug testing laboratory that helped the I.O.C. to identify athletes whose positive tests had been covered up.

Rodchenkov's lawyer said while there may have been some natural skepticism when the whistle-blower first made the claims of a widespread doping conspiracy, the chemist's credibility as a witness has been strengthened by the world's antidoping regulator, its independent investigator and now the I.O.C.

"There's overwhelming evidence showing that he's told the truth," Walden said. "At this point we would have thought FIFA would want to talk to him as one of its first priorities."

FIFA hasn't hired an independent investigator to analyze the suspected doping cases. So far no soccer samples have been analyzed by the Lausanne laboratory that developed the complex tests to detect anomalies in Russian samples. FIFA has asked for its samples to be given priority after the last of the Sochi samples are tested later this month.

Dvorak, now a consulting neurologist at Zurich's Schulthess Clinic, said FIFA needed to act quickly to avoid allowing the Russian team to play under a cloud of suspicion. Reedie, the WADA president, added that it was up to the federations to verify WADA's information and act accordingly.

"We want them to go ahead and act on this because they are responsible for the results," he said.

Madison Brengle Sues I.T.F. and WTA Over Injury From Blood Testing

BY BEN ROTHENBERG | APRIL 10, 2018

DANIEL ISLAND, S.C. — The tennis player Madison Brengle filed a lawsuit in Manatee County, Fla., circuit court on Monday afternoon against the Women's Tennis Association and the International Tennis Federation, seeking damages for battery, negligence and intentional infliction of emotional distress stemming from blood-testing procedures that she said permanently damaged her right arm.

The lawsuit also named International Doping Tests and Management, a Swedish company that administers tests for the I.T.F.; Stuart Miller, who is in charge of the I.T.F.'s antidoping program; and John Snowball, a doping control officer for I.D.T.M.

Brengle, 28, said the defendants acted with disregard for her well-being by subjecting her to vein-penetrating blood drawings for antidoping tests, despite her having a medical condition that causes extreme pain when a needle is inserted into her arm.

The I.T.F. said in a statement that the federation was aware of Brengle's accusations, but had not yet been served with the lawsuit and would not comment on it. The WTA did not respond to a request for comment.

The pain from three mandatory blood tests before Grand Slam events in 2016 has lingered, Brengle said, leaving her with damage to her right arm that has affected her serve.

Months after the last of her 2016 drug tests, Brengle was found to have complex regional pain syndrome induced by venipuncture.

In a statement, Brengle's lawyer, Peter R. Ginsberg, said his client had endured "prolonged mistreatment at the hands of the giants in women's professional tennis" and filed the suit "seeking protection from their abusive administration of the antidoping program."

According to the complaint, Brengle is seeking damages in excess of $10 million. She has won $2.2 million in prize money during her career.

In an interview last week before her lawsuit was filed, Brengle said that intense reactions to venipuncture have been an issue in her family for generations. She said that when her grandmother was in a coma after suffering a stroke, she screamed when a nurse inserted a needle into her arm.

She said she did not have issues with immunizations or other injections until she had intravenous sedation when having her wisdom teeth removed at 17.

"It felt like my arm was getting cut off," she said. "I'm screaming in pain, because I wasn't expecting that."

"It's lightning, it's acid pouring into your skin," she said of the pain.

Brengle had her first antidoping blood test at the Wimbledon qualifying tournament in 2009. She said that the phlebotomist missed the vein in her left arm twice, and that her vein collapsed on the third try.

"I hit the floor," Brengle said. "I passed out from the pain."

She was not given another blood test until 2016, before the Australian Open. Worried that the swelling and pain would leave her unable to play in the tournament, where she had reached the fourth round the year before, Brengle had the test moved up several days. She recovered and reached the third round before losing to the eventual champion Angelique Kerber.

Brengle said she had a panic attack before her next test at Wimbledon, but thought it might be better if the blood was drawn from her foot.

"I still fully didn't understand my condition," she said. "And I was so desperate to be O.K."

Brengle said that when she had "a very visible panic attack," Snowball suggested the testers "put a blindfold on her."

"To a person who is having a panic attack, to threaten to blindfold them, that's like Guantánamo Bay stuff," Brengle said through tears.

Rather than showing sympathy, she said, antidoping authorities have responded with threats to punish her for uncooperative behavior.

After the blood was drawn, Brengle's right foot badly swelled and bruised, which she documented with photos. Her next blood test, at the United States Open, caused such swelling in her arm that she was forced to retire from her first-round match. Her hand still swells and burns, she said, and she cannot feel her middle, ring or pinkie fingers.

"This is the test my body never recovered from," Brengle said. "This is the one that changed my career, changed my life, more than you can know."

Later that fall, Brengle was given a diagnosis of C.R.P.S. Though her suit contends that the defendants were "knowing and ignoring that she suffers from a rare medically-diagnosed physical condition," it does not seem that she underwent any blood tests after her diagnosis, which was verified by an I.T.F.-picked doctor.

In Brengle's complaint she said she received an agreement from Miller last August on behalf of the I.T.F. and antidoping agencies to give her "a one-year conditional exemption from venipuncture blood testing after years of Brengle's pleas and requests."

Brengle wants to extend that exemption for the remainder of her career. In the closing of the complaint she filed Monday, Brengle seeks "entry of a Permanent Injunction restraining Defendants from performing and threatening to perform a venipuncture blood test" on her.

Brengle's serve was never a primary weapon for her, but it has gotten much weaker of late.

According to Tennis Abstract, from the start of the 2015 until the 2016 U.S. Open, Brengle hit at least one ace in 48 of 72 tracked matches (66.6 percent) and won less than 50 percent of first-serve points only 10 times (13.9 percent). Since then, she has hit an ace in just 8 of 61 tracked matches (13.1 percent) and has won less than 50 percent of first serves 17 times (27.9 percent). Her serve speed has also dipped.

She has kept her ranking inside the top 100, but she has never re-entered the top 50, where she was ranked before the 2016 U.S. Open.

Despite her diminished serve and preoccupying pain, Brengle, a clever counterpuncher, has managed several upset victories since her diagnosis. In January of last year, she beat Serena Williams on a wind-swept day in Auckland. Six months later, Brengle defeated Petra Kvitova at Wimbledon, where Kvitova is a two-time champion.

"The doctors, they kept asking me: 'How do you still play professional tennis?" Brengle said. "They don't see a professional athlete with this disease, because it should shut you down."

Before the lawsuit was filed, Miller would not comment on Brengle's specific circumstances. He said some modifications were allowed in testing to make it more comfortable, including narrower needles or having the athlete lie down instead of sitting upright.

"The questions are always: what can you do to alleviate the burden of any issues a player may have while still having them comply with their obligations as a tennis player to comply with the antidoping program?" Miller said.

Brengle said she suggested alternative methods, including a suction device that pulls blood from capillaries through the skin, but Miller said that only blood from the veins had been validated for sample collection.

Blood tests have increased steadily in recent years in tennis in part because of the sport's biological passport program, which seeks to establish baseline levels for athletes that can be tracked over time.

"You can't have a robust antidoping program without collecting blood samples, because they provide additional detection methodologies that urine samples alone won't," Miller said.

In 2013, the Serbian player Viktor Troicki was given an 18-month ban, which was later reduced to 12 months, for declining a blood test at a tournament. Troicki said that he thought he could return to give the blood sample the next day without penalty.

Brengle, currently ranked 83rd, said that if she were ever forced to undergo another vein-puncturing blood test, she would retire from the sport instead.

"It would break my heart, but my health is too important," she said.

Peru's Paolo Guerrero Vows to Fight Doping Ban: 'This Is About My Honor'

BY TARIQ PANJA | MAY 18, 2018

PAOLO GUERRERO should be the happiest man in the world.

Peru, after a 36-year absence, will be at soccer's World Cup in Russia next month, and Guerrero, in the twilight of a peripatetic career, was to be there to lead the team out as its captain and star striker.

But instead of daydreaming about opening the scoring against Denmark in Saransk, the 34-year-old Guerrero is consumed with angst. A six-month drug suspension he thought he had completed was instead extended to 14 months this week, dashing his dreams but also those of a nation whose adoration for him had only grown during his exile.

Guerrero vowed to appeal the new, longer ban, a long-shot effort that quickly gained the backing of even Peru's president, Martín Vizcarra.

"This is about my honor and my family's honor," Guerrero said in a telephone interview on Friday, his voice breaking with emotion. "There are people talking about me, that I did this, but I've never done anything like this. I've never taken any drug.

"I've played for more than 15 years with dedication. I played my first game for the national team when I was 19 and always fought to reach the World Cup. I gave everything to lift my country to the tournament, and now I can't play because of something so unjust. I'm just really sad."

Yet for Guerrero, who most recently played for Brazil's biggest team, Flamengo, the biggest current concern is the effect the ban is having on the health of his parents, José and Petrolina, who are both in their 70s.

"My mom and dad are the most important people in my life," he said. "To see them so sad, so worried that they can't sleep because they can't see me live my dream — that's the worst thing."

Guerrero spoke from his home in Peru, where his mother was joined by a legal team plotting a Hail Mary appeal with Switzerland's Supreme Court to overturn the ban imposed after the Swiss-based Court of Arbitration for Sport sided with the World Anti-Doping Agency's own appeal of the six-month ban.

Guerrero insisted he was not a drug cheat, and at least two disciplinary panels have appeared to agree with him. FIFA, the world governing body of soccer, accepted his explanation for the positive test and reduced his original one-year ban to six months, a suspension that, perhaps not accidentally, would have ended just in time for him to compete in Russia. And in its decision this week, a Court of Arbitration for Sport panel said it "accepted that he did not attempt to enhance his performance by ingesting the prohibited substance."

Yet C.A.S., siding with the World Anti-Doping Agency, which had appealed the shortened ban, still ruled that Guerrero bore "some fault or negligence, even if it was not significant," as justification for extending his suspension.

Guerrero said Friday that he tested positive for traces of a cocaine derivative after drinking contaminated tea before two crucial World Cup qualification matches against Argentina and Colombia late last year. That positive test meant he was unable to play in November when Peru sealed its first qualification since 1982 by beating New Zealand in a two-game intercontinental playoff.

When Jefferson Farfán scored the first goal in the clinching game, he celebrated with the jersey of the absent Guerrero. The team's 2-0 victory sparked wild celebrations across Peru, with thousands of flag-waving supporters taking to the streets, and the government declared a public holiday the next day to mark the occasion.

While the chances of earning a reprieve are slim, Guerrero, whose 32 career goals are a Peru record, said he would live up to his name and not give up until the very end.

"I'm a fighter," he said. "I've always fought when the road has been difficult. It's not easy to become a professional footballer. I fought to become one. I'll keep fighting, keep demonstrating my innocence, do everything in my hands to play in the World Cup. I'm not going to let my head drop and just go to my bed and lie down."

FIFPro, the global players' union, has joined the legal battle to overturn Guerrero's suspension. It is urging doping authorities to reconsider regulations that leave no room for mitigating factors in the cases of athletes like Guerrero, even when disciplinary panels acknowledge they ingested banned substances through no fault of their own.

"Both FIFA and the Court of Arbitration for Sport agreed Guerrero did not knowingly ingest the substance and that there was no performance-enhancing effect," FIFPro said in a statement. "It therefore defies common sense that he should be handed a punishment which is so damaging to his career."

Guerrero, like the rest of his Peru teammates, was not yet born the last time his country made an appearance at the World Cup, in Spain in 1982. And he said that he recognized that Russia was almost certainly his last chance to fulfill a childhood dream, of getting that feeling in the pit of his stomach before a big match, of easing José and Petrolina's pain, as well as that of more than 30 million of his countrymen.

"Football is my life, my passion, and this is my biggest dream," he said. "Don't take it away."

For Tennis Players, Numbers in Antidoping Program Don't Add Up

BY KAREN CROUSE | JULY 3, 2018

WIMBLEDON, ENGLAND — Serena Williams expressed no qualms about antidoping officers showing up unannounced to collect urine and, on occasion, blood samples. She wasn't even bothered when it happened twice in the same week in the lead-up to this year's French Open. It was like T.S.A. searches at the airport — a minor inconvenience of her high-flying tennis career.

The five out-of-competition tests in the first six months of 2018 didn't irritate Williams until she saw numbers, plucked from the United States Anti-Doping Agency's public database and included in a recent Deadspin article, that seemed to suggest she was being tested far more often than her compatriots in the sport.

CLIVE MASON/GETTY IMAGES

Serena Williams, serving at Wimbledon in 2018, doesn't understand why she gets tested for performance-enhancing drugs so often. Other players have similar questions.

The registered pool of performers included the United States Open champion Sloane Stephens and the finalist she beat, Madison Keys, who were listed as having one completed test, and Sam Querrey, the men's world No. 13, who had none.

"I didn't know I was being tested three times more — in some cases five times more — than everyone else," Williams said Monday after her straight-sets victory over Arantxa Rus in the first round at Wimbledon.

Williams wasn't alone in feeling aggrieved. When Keys heard about Williams's five tests, she said, "My first thought was why has she only gotten tested five times when I've gotten tested eight or nine times."

In the sweltering heat that has made southwest London in July feel like southwest Ohio, drug testing has become the mosquito buzzing around the All-England Club, making many players irritable and itching for a fight.

"I really want answers," Williams said. "Like, then you hear people complaining about they don't get tested. I'm like, 'Well, you know ...' "

It turns out that drug testing is a puzzle for which no athlete holds all the pieces, precluding any of them from seeing the complete picture. Deadspin didn't have all the information.

Williams, for example, didn't know that Keys had submitted to several out-of-competition tests administered by an antidoping program operating under the auspices of the International Tennis Federation. And neither Williams nor Keys was aware that United States Anti-Doping Agency, or Usada, keeps a record of all completed tests in a public database that does not include the less transparent I.T.F. program results.

It's as if Usada, in its pursuit of full transparency, has created a false positive, sowing a climate of wariness and confusion among elite athletes instead of an atmosphere of trust and confidence.

Travis Tygart, the chief executive officer of Usada, said the Deadspin article had spurred a great discussion.

"I'm glad athletes are engaging in it," he said Monday by telephone.

Nobody's purposes are being served, he added, "if there is no level of accountability or when people are making false conclusions based on a partial picture."

For American athletes in other Olympic sports, the testing numbers in tennis seem incomprehensibly incomplete. The long-distance runner Kara Goucher noted that she submitted to 17 out-of-competition Usada tests in 2016, the year she narrowly missed a third Olympic berth. That same year, Williams had six.

"To be honest, I'm kind of shocked by those tennis numbers," Goucher said by telephone.

Alluding to Williams's career earnings of more than $84.8 million, Goucher added: "I'm just surprised there isn't more testing in a sport where there's so much more money than in track and field. As someone who has used Serena as an example of an athlete who has inspired me, I'd tell her, 'You should want the testing to be as rigorous as it can be."

Tennis players would prefer a random system of out-of-competition testing in which names are spit out of a machine like lottery balls. Giving voice to the prevailing sentiment, Williams said, "Just test everyone equally."

With finite resources to catch athletes who are cheating and deter any who might be considering it, Usada opts for testing that is reasonable if not random. Tygart said athletes were selected for testing based on an algorithm that assesses internationally established risk factors, like performance improvement, ranking, biological analysis, the competition calendar, injury and research on doping trends.

To that list, the athletes would tack on one more factor: geography. Roger Federer, who maintains homes in Switzerland and Dubai, said that he had been tested once in the past 15 years at his residence in the Middle East and laughably often when he is living near Basel, his hometown.

"The tester lives in the same village, so it's very convenient," Federer said. "If he's bored at home, he probably just says, 'Let me check in on Roger to see if he's having a good time.' "

Federer laughed. "Maybe that's the part I don't like so much," he added. "The inconsistency of the places where they test."

Tennis players' peripatetic lifestyle can turn drug testing into a global game of tag. Consider Keys, who when she is not competing can be found at her Florida home or with her California-based coach or with her Iowa-based mother.

"When I'm in the middle of nowhere, in Iowa when I'm at my mom's, I don't get tested quite as often as when I'm in Florida or L.A.," she said.

Bob Bryan, like Williams, lives outside Miami, and he has historically been tested more often than his identical twin and doubles partner, Mike, who lives in sleepy Camarillo, Calif., an hour outside Los Angeles. This year Bob, who has been sidelined with a hip injury since mid-May, is listed as having completed four Usada tests to Mike's two. Bob has 56 career tests, more than Mike (43), Williams (41) or Williams's sister Venus (43).

"I think I am tested more frequently because I live in a big city and am a very convenient option for drug testers," Bob wrote in an email.

The Usada protocol requires athletes to provide a daily one-hour window in which they must be available for drug testing. In addition, athletes can be subjected to extended tests, which are administered outside the scheduled 60-minute window and are meant to deter anyone from manipulating the data in a biological passport through micro-dosing or other methods.

"In the past I have walked a drug tester to my front door only to be greeted by another from a different organization," Bryan said, adding, "I am strongly in favor of organizations helping to keep our sport clean, but when I continually have to open my front door to unannounced testing agents, at times I feel it is a bit excessive."

Tygart said Usada's continuing logistical challenge was to allocate its resources efficiently and effectively. "Obviously, we don't want athletes to feel like there's ever a loophole in terms of there being any location where they won't be tested," he said.

American antidoping officials aim to avoid multiple testing situations like the one Bryan described by tracking the completed tests administered by the international sports federations. But as much as Usada aims to work around other tests, the lag time between the administering of the tests and the filing of the results to the World Anti-Doping Agency makes some gaps in information inevitable.

Querrey grew indignant upon hearing that the Usada database had credited him with no completed out-of-competition tests this year.

After advancing to the semifinals of Wimbledon and the quarterfinals of the United States Open last year and ascending to a career-best No. 11 in the rankings in February, Querrey figured he would be targeted more frequently for tests. And he insisted that he had been.

"I've probably been tested at my house this year seven times," Querrey said, adding, "I feel like I get tested at home eight to 10 times a year and at tournaments 10 times a year. It's a ton."

The Usada numbers don't reflect out-of-competition tests administered by tennis' antidoping program or in-competition tests at tournaments. Further complicating the picture, one visit could result in two test results if blood and urine samples are collected.

It is conceivable that Usada officials, after noting the frequency with which Querrey is being tested outside of competition by tennis' antidoping program, shifted their focus to other players, including Williams, who had a child last year and has played very few tournaments.

Querrey's commitment to clean sport is for the life of his career, which is why he set aside one hour in the morning, as usual, for Usada collection officers to test him the day he was married to the model Abby Dixon in Florida last month. To Querrey's relief, no uninvited guests crashed his wedding.

Did Flawed Data Lead Track Astray on Testosterone in Women?

BY JERÉ LONGMAN | JULY 12, 2018

RESEARCHERS HAVE FOUND flaws in some of the data that track and field officials used to formulate regulations for the complicated cases of Caster Semenya of South Africa, the two-time Olympic champion at 800 meters, and other female athletes with naturally elevated testosterone levels.

Three independent researchers said they believed the mistakes called into question the validity of a 2017 study commissioned by track and field's world governing body, the International Federation of Athletics Associations, or I.A.A.F., according to interviews and a paper written by the researchers and provided to The New York Times.

The 2017 study was used to help devise regulations that could require some runners to undergo medical treatment to lower their hormone levels to remain eligible for the sport's most prominent international competitions, like the Summer Games.

The researchers have called for a retraction of the study, published last year in the British Journal of Sports Medicine. The study served as an underpinning for rules, scheduled to be enacted in November, which would establish permitted testosterone levels for athletes participating in women's events from 400 meters to the mile.

"They cannot use this study as an excuse or a reason for setting a testosterone level because the data they have presented is not solid," one of the independent researchers, Erik Boye of Norway, said Thursday.

The I.A.A.F. has updated its research, which was published last week, again in the British Journal of Sports Medicine. "The I.A.A.F. will not be seeking a retraction of the 2017 study," the governing body said in a statement on Thursday. "The conclusions remain the same."

But the statement did little to dampen criticism by the independent researchers. The I.A.A.F. seems "bound to lose" an intended challenge by Semenya to the Court of Arbitration for Sport, a kind of Supreme Court for international athletics, said Boye, a cancer researcher and an antidoping expert.

The I.A.A.F. has argued for years that rules governing testosterone levels are needed to level the playing field and to reduce an unfair advantage gained in some women's events by athletes with so-called differences of sexual development. The 2017 study was only one facet of 15 years' worth of field study, the I.A.A.F. said.

Dr. Stephane Bermon, the I.A.A.F.'s senior medical and scientific consultant and a co-author of the 2017 study, last week acknowledged some errors in the data in an email sent to one of the independent researchers. But Dr. Bermon added in the email, obtained by The Times, that the mistakes "do not have significant impact on the final outcomes and conclusions of our study."

Karim Khan, editor in chief of the British Journal of Sports Medicine, did not respond to emails seeking comment.

The disputed 2017 study in the journal examined results from the 2011 and 2013 world track and field championships. It found that women with the highest testosterone levels significantly outperformed women with the lowest testosterone levels in events such as the 400 meters, the 400-meter hurdles and the 800 meters, which distill speed and endurance.

But in examining the study's results from those three races, plus the 1,500 meters, the three independent researchers said they found that the performance data used in the study's analysis was anomalous or inaccurate 17 percent to 33 percent of the time.

The errors included more than one time recorded for the same athlete; repeated use of the same time for individual athletes; and phantom times when no athlete could be found to have run a reported time. Also included were times for athletes who were disqualified for doping.

"I think everyone can understand that if your data set is contaminated by as much as one-third bad data, it's kind of a garbage-in, garbage-out situation," said one of the independent researchers, Roger

Pielke Jr., the director of the Sports Governance Center at the University of Colorado.

Referring to the I.A.A.F., Pielke said: "I really see no option for them other than to retract the paper. If they retract the paper, then the regulations don't have a scientific basis."

After reading the revised study on Thursday, Pielke noted that the I.A.A.F. was now acknowledging there were 220 errors in performance data found across every women's track and field event at the 2011 and 2013 world championships.

"This is an effort at what I would call a do-over, and it's embarrassing and it's not how science is expected to be done," Pielke said. "I think this adds considerably more weight to our call for the original paper to be retracted. This is everything but putting up a billboard saying, 'We really screwed up the data in the original study.' "

Another of the independent researchers, Ross Tucker, an exercise physiologist who specializes in sports performance at the University of Cape Town in South Africa, agreed that the first study should still be retracted. The re-analysis, he said, included "too much uncertainty to trust."

A re-analysis of the original study might, in fact, make even a stronger case for the I.A.A.F.'s position on the need to regulate testosterone levels, the independent researchers said in interviews. But any new analysis should be conducted only with a full independent audit and with publicly available performance data that could be replicated by independent scholars, the researchers said.

The I.A.A.F. has lacked transparency in providing and presenting its data, said Boye, the Norwegian researcher, who described the governing body as "doing everything with their hands over the data."

Given the data errors, the original study is "entirely untrustworthy" and "an impossible position" for the I.A.A.F. to defend, said Tucker, the South African researcher.

He added, "If I was on Semenya's team, this would be among the best news I could receive."

If the challenge to the study succeeds, this would be the second major setback for the I.A.A.F. in trying to set testosterone limits.

In 2015, the Court of Arbitration for Sport suspended a previous I.A.A.F. rule, saying the governing body had not sufficiently quantified the performance advantage gained in women's events by elevated testosterone levels. That case involved an Indian sprinter named Dutee Chand.

The challenge to the 2017 study is the second time this week that the I.A.A.F. has come under criticism. More than 60 current and former elite athletes, including the tennis legend Billie Jean King and the soccer champions Abby Wambach and Megan Rapinoe, signed an open letter in support of Semenya, calling for the pending testosterone rules to be rescinded.

The athletes described the regulations as discriminatory and invasive, arguing that "no woman should be required to change her body to compete in women's sport."

But the I.A.A.F. has said that, in some events, athletes with differences of sexual development could have a performance advantage of 5 percent to 6 percent over athletes with testosterone in the typical female range, an enormous difference in a sport where events can be decided by hundredths of a second.

The pending rules would affect women with testosterone levels of five nanomoles per liter and above. Most women, including elite athletes, have natural testosterone levels of .12 to 1.79 nanomoles per liter, the I.A.A.F. said, while the typical male range after puberty is much higher, at 7.7 to 29.4 nanomoles per liter.

No female athlete would have natural testosterone levels at five nanomoles per liter or higher without so-called differences in sex development or tumors, the I.A.A.F. said. In effect, it has said that athletes with such elevated levels are biologically male.

But the scientific discussion has now been somewhat sidetracked by questions about the independence and validity of the I.A.A.F.'s research.

"You don't have drug companies doing their own studies that no one else can see," Pielke, the Colorado researcher, said.

CHAPTER 6

Antidoping and the Future

Attempts to regulate doping in sports have run up against the efforts of organizations that benefit from continuing to adjust athletes' body chemistry to eke out more efficient performances. As such doping schemes have become more sophisticated, so have efforts to combat them, like the use of biological passports. While lawmakers seek to criminalize doping, illegal drugs flourish on the black market, and science continues to develop new, potentially dangerous performance-enhancing drugs. Time will tell whether laws aimed at combating doping prove successful.

Antidoping Authorities From 17 Nations Push for a Series of Reforms

BY REBECCA R. RUIZ | AUG. 30, 2016

WITH THE RIO OLYMPICS having barely concluded, antidoping authorities from 17 countries met in Copenhagen this week and pushed ahead with a series of proposals, including one that would prohibit any antidoping employee from having an overlapping leadership role in international sports.

That would "prevent the inherent conflict of interest that exists when a sports organization is tasked with both promoting and policing itself," the authorities said, indirectly criticizing global sports' top antidoping official, who is also a top Olympic official.

The officials — representing countries including Australia, Canada and the United States — also called for term limits for antidoping officials; increased funding for the World Anti-Doping Agency, from a source other than the International Olympic Committee; and additional sanctions for Russia in the wake of revelations of state-sponsored doping.

"We hope this is a constructive contribution to the reform that is needed," said Joseph de Pencier, the founding chief executive of the Institute of National Anti-Doping Organizations and among those at the Copenhagen meeting.

"I don't think we ever imagined you could have a state-run doping program that would subvert antidoping controls," Mr. de Pencier said in a telephone interview on Tuesday. "We've got to detect it, deter it and sanction it — so it doesn't ruin sport."

Expressing support for a continuing investigation into Russian doping, the officials at the Copenhagen session requested reparations for athletes who had been harmed by doping violations and compensation for Russian whistle-blowers who have fled the country.

The I.O.C., WADA and individual sports organizations have the authority to act on the recommendations that come out of the Copenhagen meeting. The I.O.C. has scheduled a summit meeting for Oct. 8 in Switzerland that will focus on improving the global antidoping system. World antidoping officials are expected to meet in September and November.

Mr. de Pencier said antidoping officials wanted to emphasize support for WADA, which was heavily criticized by Olympic committee members in Rio de Janeiro this month, while making clear that significant aspects of its structure and governance needed to change.

In shaping their proposed reforms this week, the array of antidoping officials — many of whom had banded together earlier in the summer to agitate for barring Russia from the Olympics — said they hoped to "restore confidence in the integrity of international sport, which has been deeply damaged, and ensure that the disturbing events of recent years are not repeated."

An inquiry seeking to determine which Russian athletes may have benefited from the nation's doping system is underway, and the president of the I.O.C., Thomas Bach, said in Rio this month that, once that inquiry has concluded, the committee would have to consider "disqualification, reallocation of medals, exclusion from future Games."

At least 15 Russian medalists from the Sochi Games doped throughout the competition, Russia's former antidoping lab chief said last spring. As of this month, the athletes in question have retained those medals.

Russian whistle-blowers, meanwhile, have expressed concerns for their safety. "It seems WADA told us be safe, and let the cheaters win," said Vitaly Stepanov, a former employee of Russia's antidoping agency who left Russia in 2014 after he and his wife, Yuliya, a middle-distance runner, made their knowledge of Russia's doping system public.

The I.O.C. denied Mrs. Stepanova entry to the Rio Games, overruling track and field officials who had voted to include her as a neutral competitor rather than one representing Russia.

Mrs. Stepanova said this month that she thought the Olympic officials' decision would have a chilling effect on other whistle-blowers. "If you open your mouth, you will never be an Olympic athlete," she said.

In their Copenhagen proposal, the antidoping officials asked the I.O.C. and Russia to "do everything in their power to protect and ensure safety, security and a sustainable future" for the Stepanovs and other whistle-blowers.

In Rio this month, Mr. Bach said the Olympic committee was "not responsible for dangers to which Mrs. Stepanova may be exposed," adding, "We nevertheless expressed our appreciation for her great contribution to the fight against doping."

Travis Tygart, the president of the United States Anti-Doping agency and among the officials who participated in this week's meeting, said a rule prohibiting overlapping leadership positions in sports and antidoping organizations was one of the most important reforms that could be enacted. It is aimed at divorcing sports leadership — and possible financial interests in sports competitions — from the people responsible for rooting out drug violations that are capable of tarnishing those competitions.

This week's proposal would forbid employees or decision-makers of any antidoping agency to have simultaneous policy-making ties to the I.O.C. or any other sports organization.

The current top global official in the fight against doping — Craig Reedie, president of the WADA — is also an executive board member of the I.O.C.

"We have to remove the conflict of interest," Mr. Tygart said, "and ensure that the fox is no longer allowed to guard the hen house."

Hall of Fame Voters Soften Stance on Stars of Steroids Era

BY DAVID WALDSTEIN | JAN. 2, 2017

BARRY BONDS and Roger Clemens, two of the most successful players in baseball history, are among the former stars who were essentially blacklisted from the Hall of Fame because of their reputations as doping cheats. But now it appears that such players might end up enshrined in Cooperstown after all.

In a sudden and surprising shift of sentiment, the baseball writers who vote to decide who should be inducted into the Hall, and who should not, appear to be backing away from their punitive approach to Bonds and Clemens, and perhaps others as well.

Were Bonds and Clemens to actually end up in the Hall, it would be a striking moment for the sport and its millions of fans. No team sport in the United States has as much tradition as baseball does, nor does any other sport have a Hall of Fame that carries nearly as much prestige as the one in Cooperstown.

And no team sport in this country has been as vexed by the issue of doping as baseball has. For better or worse, baseball has often served as the American battleground over the issue of doping, with the sport's officials slow to confront the problem during the so-called steroid era and then eventually becoming more aggressive than other leagues in cracking down.

All of this created considerable anguish in baseball and a seeming consensus that even players as good as Bonds, the career leader in home runs, and Clemens, an intimidating strikeout artist who won a colossal 354 games, should be kept out of the Hall if they were directly linked to performance-enhancing drugs.

But that consensus is cracking. Part of the reason is that the hundreds of writers who vote are, as a whole, becoming younger and seemingly less inclined to take an unyielding stance on steroid cheats.

And part of the reason appears to be the decision last month to induct Bud Selig into the Hall. Selig, who served as commissioner of baseball as the record books were being obliterated by bulked-up players, was granted entry into Cooperstown by a veterans' committee that is separate from the writers' bloc.

Selig had long been criticized for failing to combat the doping scourge sooner. Now he was headed to Cooperstown, joining, among others, the former manager Tony La Russa, who was inducted in 2014 and who oversaw a number of highly successful teams that benefited from the presence of steroid users.

All of it "just kind of struck a nerve with me," said Kevin Cooney, a voter from The Courier Times in Bucks County, Pa.

"To me, it would be hypocritical to put the commissioner of the steroid era and a manager who had connections with the steroid era in and leave out the greatest pitcher and the greatest hitter of that time," Cooney said in explaining why he had now decided to vote for Bonds and Clemens.

Another writer, Susan Slusser of The San Francisco Chronicle, posted a pointed message on social media after Selig's induction. In it, Slusser, a former president of the Baseball Writers' Association of America, said the induction had now compelled her to reconsider how she would vote on this year's ballot for the Hall.

She argued that if Selig was being inducted, it was "senseless" to keep out players who were accused of using drugs.

As a longtime beat writer for The Chronicle, Slusser is well respected by her fellow writers. Her statement got their attention and seemed to contribute to the shift now taking place.

"There is nothing good about the whole era," Slusser said in a telephone interview. "And I just decided that if you honor the central figures of the era — the execs and managers and players and media people are all going in — then it's putting the entire wrongs of that era on two guys."

Other voters clearly share Slusser and Cooney's thinking, and that shift is reflected in the vote totals tabulated on Ryan Thibodaux's BBHOF ballot tracker, which lists Hall of Fame ballots that writers have made public in advance of the announcement of the final vote totals later this month.

Of the more than 150 voters who have taken the public route — representing a little over a third of the electorate — 21 voted for Bonds for the first time after previously declining to do so, and 22 did the same for Clemens.

That growing support has left Bonds and Clemens closing in on the 75 percent threshold needed for induction. As of Monday evening, each had been named on 111 of the 158 ballots on Thibodaux's site, or 70.3 percent.

Based on previous voting patterns, the percentages for Bonds and Clemens are expected to come down some — to somewhere above 60 percent — when all the votes are tabulated. Still, a pathway to induction has come into focus for the two men midway through their 10 years of ballot eligibility.

Last year, Clemens received 45.2 percent of the vote and Bonds 44.3. It was the best they had done to date, but still far short of where they needed to get. But if they can get over 60 percent this time, with five more years left on the ballot, they may pick up enough momentum to eventually get the necessary three-quarters of the vote. Other players have followed a similar trajectory into the Hall.

Then again, other players do not carry the baggage that Bonds and Clemens do. Not only were they linked to illicit drugs, but both ended up facing criminal charges that they lied about their drug use in legal settings.

Bonds was charged with perjury and obstruction of justice for statements he made before a federal grand jury and was initially convicted of the latter charge before the verdict was overturned. Clemens, whose denial of drug use led to a nationally televised hearing before a congressional panel, was ultimately acquitted of perjury and other charges in a federal trial.

But even with all those unsettling facts to consider, some writers are changing their minds.

Steve Buckley of The Boston Herald said he pictured himself sitting in the audience at Cooperstown for future induction ceremonies and looking out at Selig and La Russa and others who he said benefited from the steroid era and wondering why the two best players of the time were barred.

"I'm not saying Bud turned a blind eye to it or that he knew it was happening," Buckley said of the drug use under Selig's watch. "I'm simply saying that Clemens and Bonds and others took the performance-enhancing drugs and did the steroids and all those evil things, and at the end of the day, the game did prosper, and they are on the outside looking in, and I have an issue with that."

But then there is Gordon Wittenmyer of The Chicago Sun-Times, who did not vote for Bonds or Clemens this time, either, and who said that comparing Selig to the two former stars did not make sense.

He recalled that before his first vote a few years ago, when another tainted slugger, Mark McGwire, was still on the ballot, he described the voting process to his son, who was 12 at the time. Wittenmyer described each player's biography and what he had seen from them up close as a writer. Then he explained the steroid issue.

"His response was, 'Well, Dad, isn't that cheating?' And I said, 'Yeah, it was,' " Wittenmyer said. "If that's the easy conclusion a 12-year-old draws, it really is that simple." But how many voters still feel like Wittenmyer has become an intriguing question.

Antidoping Officials Get an Earful from Congress: 'What a Broken System'

BY REBECCA R. RUIZ | FEB. 28, 2017

WASHINGTON — Federal lawmakers excoriated international sports officials on Tuesday for what they called a bungled response to the Russian doping scandal, with delayed investigations, insufficient sanctions and a lack of interest in rooting out cheating that has tarnished the Olympic brand.

During a two-hour hearing called by a House subcommittee, Democrats and Republicans chastised representatives of the International Olympic Committee and the World Anti-Doping Agency, the regulator of drugs in sports.

"What a broken system," Representative Greg Walden, Republican of Oregon and chairman of the House Energy and Commerce Committee, said, asking why WADA — to which the United States is the largest national contributor — took years to act on the multiple whistle-blower tips it had received from within Russia, pursuing investigations only after news media reports.

"It's been a quagmire," Mr. Walden said, criticizing officials' "indecisive and inconsistent" responses to revelations that some 1,000 Russian athletes were implicated in state-sponsored doping schemes.

Representatives of WADA and the I.O.C. spoke little, weathering relentless criticism with few rebuttals. "At these sort of things, you're always a little frustrated you can't say more," Richard Budgett, the I.O.C.'s medical and scientific director, said as he prepared to depart.

Rob Koehler, the deputy director general of WADA, defended the organization's response to the scandal, pointing to the independent investigations it had ultimately commissioned, which amassed evidence of

DOUG MILLS/THE NEW YORK TIMES

From left, the Olympic shot-putter Adam Nelson; the Olympic swimmer Michael Phelps; and Travis Tygart, the United States' top antidoping official, being sworn in before testifying at a House subcommittee hearing in February 2017. Beyond Tygart, from left, are Rob Koehler, deputy director of the World Anti-Doping Agency, and Richard Budgett, medical and scientific director of the International Olympic Committee.

the vast scope of Russia's cheating that the I.O.C. and others are continuing to review.

WADA's president, Craig Reedie, is a member of the I.O.C.; until August, he was a top executive with that organization as well.

"If you continue to have sport overseeing investigations, overseeing compliance, overseeing itself — it's the fox guarding the henhouse," Travis Tygart, the United States' top antidoping official, told the subcommittee.

Mr. Tygart invoked an array of global reforms that he and a coalition of other national antidoping organizations had proposed in August. Most of all, he advocated making the global antidoping regulator more independent of sports organizations, empowering it to be an aggressive policeman.

The United States Olympic Committee, which is politicking to host the 2024 Summer Games, had argued against holding a hearing last year, when Mr. Tygart and antidoping authorities from more than a dozen other nations were pressuring the I.O.C. to ban Russia from the 2016 Games after learning the nation's antidoping lab chief had tampered with scores of urine samples at the 2014 Sochi Olympics.

Representative Tim Murphy — Republican of Pennsylvania and the chairman of the subcommittee on oversight and investigations, which called the hearing — said Tuesday that the inquiry was justified and that Congress's concern went beyond its $2 million annual contribution to the global regulator.

"It isn't just the money the United States puts into this," Mr. Murphy said. "If it takes money to motivate things, fine, but the real reason is: I want sports to be fair." He said he also considered doping a public health issue.

Testifying alongside the sports and antidoping authorities were two American Olympic medalists, the swimmer Michael Phelps and the shot-putter Adam Nelson, who told personal anecdotes. Some lawmakers took photographs of the athletes before and after the charged discussion.

Mr. Phelps, the world's most decorated Olympian, said he did not believe that he had ever competed in a clean field, and he echoed Mr. Tygart's calls for making the antidoping regulator more independent.

Mr. Nelson — who inherited a gold medal roughly a decade after he had competed, once a reporter had informed him that a competitor had been disqualified for doping — said he wanted to ensure officials would not "sweep this under the rug."

He was presented with his gold medal in the food court of an Atlanta airport, a fact numerous representatives seized on, arguing for a ceremony to honor the dozens of athletes who have retroactively won medals because of the rash of doping disqualifications over the last year.

Diana DeGette, Democrat of Colorado, drew parallels between Tuesday's proceeding and hearings called in the early 2000s by the same subcommittee regarding the Salt Lake Olympics corruption scandal, in which American officials had bribed I.O.C. members to win the right to host the 2002 Games.

After reading excerpts from an I.O.C. letter on the Russian doping scandal released last week, Ms. DeGette said, “This is the same kind of gobbledygook we got from the I.O.C. then.”

In the letter, addressed to various sports organizations, the I.O.C. had sought to differentiate between calling Russia’s widespread cheating “state-sponsored” and “institutional,” a major point of contention for Russian sports officials who have emphasized that President Vladimir V. Putin and his inner circle were not involved in the coordinated cheating.

“They’re looking at angels dancing on the head of a pin, and I don’t even know what they’re talking about,” Ms. DeGette said. “The international sports community needs to realize we’re dealing with Russia and the honor system is simply not going to be enough.”

Russian Hackers Release Stolen Emails in New Effort to Undermine Doping Investigators

BY REBECCA R. RUIZ | JAN. 10, 2018

A RUSSIAN CYBERESPIONAGE GROUP that has made international athletes a top target published a new set of stolen emails on Wednesday, seeking to highlight discord among global sports officials and the antidoping investigators who deconstructed Russia's systematic doping.

The cyberespionage group — known as Fancy Bear and linked to Russia's main military intelligence unit, the G.R.U. — called the communications evidence of "sports officials' tension over the fight for power and cash," pointing to antidoping authorities' desire for independence from Olympic officials.

In one internal message released Wednesday, a top lawyer for the International Olympic Committee criticized the World Anti-Doping Agency, the global regulator of drugs in sports, for having published two damning investigative reports about the Russian doping scandal without having first discussed their content with sports officials.

"It seems that RM's first report was intended to lead to the complete expulsion of the Russian team from the Rio Games," the lawyer, Howard Stupp, wrote, referring to the sports investigator Richard McLaren. Mr. McLaren spent nearly a year investigating Russia's widespread cheating and ultimately produced two voluminous reports in 2016, but did not recommend specific sanctions.

"And the second report? To expulse the Russian team from the Pyeongchang Games?" Mr. Stupp wrote, referring to the coming 2018 Winter Olympics, which begin Feb. 9. "This put the I.O.C.," as well as the officials overseeing each sport and the Olympic movement in general, he wrote, "in a very difficult position."

A spokesman for the International Olympic Committee declined to comment on the communications published Wednesday. Mr. McLaren did not immediately respond to a request for his reaction to the leaked emails.

Last month, the organization banned the Russian Federation from the 2018 Winter Games but left the door open for individual Russian athletes to compete as neutrals. While it has not yet been determined just how many Russian athletes will clear the bar for competition, some critics who advocated a blanket ban on Russian athletes have cautioned that the punishment could have too many loopholes and enable Russia to send a sizable delegation.

Much of the information published Wednesday was unsurprising, reflecting routine logistical discussions among investigators, lawyers and Olympic staff members regarding, for example, the retesting of urine samples from the 2012 London Games and the 2014 Sochi Games, where Russia cheated most elaborately.

Fancy Bear emphasized, however, that some of the investigators who had worked to expose the details of Russia's cheating also had done work for the United States and British governments. As examples, the hackers pointed to Martin Dubbey, who worked with Mr. McLaren, and David Tinsley, the chief executive of 5 Stones intelligence and a former agent for the Drug Enforcement Administration. Neither man immediately responded to a request for comment on Wednesday.

Some antidoping officials said that while the hackers might have intended to embarrass or expose them, the information only underscored their efforts to disentangle the jobs of sports officials — who are tasked with promoting competitions and making them profitable — from the work of drug-testing officials working to root out cheating that damages the brand image of those competitions.

"If anything it shows what we've said since Day 1 of our existence: You can't both promote and police," Travis T. Tygart, the chief executive of the United States Anti-Doping Agency, said Wednesday.

"You have to have independent organizations handling antidoping operations."

Fancy Bear first published the private medical records of Western athletes — a majority of them American and British — in the summer of 2016, at the peak of the Russian doping scandal. Those medical records, reflecting that certain athletes had received special medical permission to use banned medications, sought to discredit the athletes in question, none of whom had committed a violation, sports officials said.

Last year, American intelligence officials published a declassified report linking Fancy Bear to Russia's main military intelligence unit, the G.R.U., and attributing to the group hacks of both the World Anti-Doping Agency and the Democratic National Committee.

"The genuine intentions of the coalition headed by the Anglo-Saxons are much less noble than a war against doping," the Russian hackers wrote on their website, echoing Russian officials' repeated claims of Western conspiracies seeking to undermine Russia and calling Mr. McLaren's investigation of Russian sports cheating "a smoke screen for special agents."

"It is apparent that the Americans and the Canadians are eager to remove the Europeans from the leadership in the Olympic movement," they wrote, "to achieve political dominance of the English-speaking nations."

Enough. Give Russia Its Flag Back, Then Make Real Changes.

BY JULIET MACUR | FEB. 22, 2018

PYEONGCHANG, SOUTH KOREA — Now that the Pyeongchang Olympics are almost over, the International Olympic Committee has to decide whether Russia has done enough penance for its state-sponsored doping program to march with its flag in the closing ceremony on Sunday.

It is not an abstract question. The Russians were here, after all: The country had nearly 170 athletes competing as neutrals under the opposite-of-neutral label of Olympic athletes from Russia. But the hand-wringing about the flag has grown tiresome.

Will the Russia team remain in exile or not? Could a partial ban solve the problem, in which the Russians would be allowed to wear official team uniforms bearing the flag, yet still be barred from carrying the flag? Could they carry the flag, but wear neutral uniforms? What's next? Official Russian uniform jackets, but neutral pants? Neutral jackets, but Russian-flag-themed pants? A Russian flag, but one only half the regular size?

Enough of this farce. Just give the Russians their flag back. And then let's start talking about the real issue:

The International Olympic Committee's plan for showing the Russians who's the boss has — most likely on purpose — lacked teeth from the start.

What the organization needs is a tangible plan that could once and for all take antidoping responsibilities away from nations like Russia — but not only Russia — that in so many cases have shown a predisposition toward looking the other way on doping, especially when it comes to their own athletes. It needs to create an independent worldwide antidoping task force, with enough financing behind it to make it work.

The I.O.C. will have to demand that all national Olympic committees and sports federations pitch in, but it needs to reach deeper into its

HILARY SWIFT FOR THE NEW YORK TIMES

The Olympic flag — rather than the Russian flag — was raised at a medal ceremony in Pyeongchang, South Korea in February 2018.

own pockets, too. NBC Universal has committed nearly $8 billion for the media rights for the Games from 2021 through 2032. That's a lot of money for the I.O.C. to throw around, and right now seems like the right time to throw a lot more of it at antidoping.

Ahead of these Winter Games, the I.O.C. talked a big talk to clean up Olympic sports, yet allowed Russia to send one of the largest contingents to these Games, and then approved a "neutral" uniform with the word "Russia" on it.

So what's the sense in letting the I.O.C. pretend to be a hard-liner on doping now that the Games are almost done by keeping the Russian flag out of the closing ceremony? The fact that it's even considering reinstatement, or the laughable partial reinstatement options, shows it still isn't serious about punishing nations that cheat to win.

Russians won 13 medals through the first 13 days of the Games. None were gold, though that is likely to change when the women's figure skating is decided Friday morning here. But the Russians were awarded four silvers and nine bronzes, and that's still something.

But you can't help but wonder, given Russia's history, if some of the athletes who finished behind them were robbed again. We know at least two Norwegians who've already had their medal moment stolen.

They blame Alexander Krushelnytsky, a Russian curler. When Krushelnytsky, a bronze medalist in mixed doubles curling, tested positive here for the banned drug meldonium, he at first denied taking the drug. Russian officials claimed sabotage, an unoriginal excuse. Elite athletes here keep close tabs on what they eat and drink, and they don't leave their water bottles just anywhere.

"I think having a Russian that has tested positive is not a good thing," said Angela Ruggiero, the chairwoman of the I.O.C.'s athletes' commission and a four-time Olympian in hockey. "Obviously we don't want any athletes testing positive, but in this particular situation, where they're under a microscope, it does raise questions."

On Thursday, Krushelnytsky stopped fighting his case and abandoned his appeal. He and his teammate will lose their bronze medals, dropping Russia to just 12 medals won here. And while the Norwegians who finished fourth will get those bronzes, they said this week that they still felt "robbed of their moment of glory."

So after a positive drug test, why is the I.O.C. even debating whether Russia should march under its flag on Sunday? Sam Edney, a Canadian luger, said the Russian curler's doping positive should guarantee that the Russian flag never waves inside the stadium. He has reason to be annoyed.

Edney was part of a team that finished fourth in Sochi, while a Russian team won silver. The Russian squad was later stripped of the medal for doping, meaning Edney and the Canadians would move up to bronze. But then the silver medal was reinstated just before these Games after the Russians won an appeal.

Edney's roller coaster is one no athlete should be forced to ride. The I.O.C., he wrote on Twitter, "needs to make a statement that enough is enough."

The Russians celebrated in Sochi, and they will celebrate here, too. They have been waving their flag in the stands and painting "Russia" on their faces.

Russian journalists showed up at figure skating this week wearing T-shirts that said, "I Don't Do Doping," even as the evidence clearly showed that, actually, Russians did "do doping." Again.

Maybe they should let the whole Russian team wear those shirts on Sunday. Let them march in their Russian uniforms behind a Russian flag held high.

It would be a perfect symbol of how much the I.O.C. seems to value clean sport.

Clashing Agendas: Antidoping Officials vs. U.S. Olympics Leaders

BY REBECCA R. RUIZ | FEB. 27, 2017

COLORADO SPRINGS — Executives at the United States Anti-Doping Agency here are agitating for a forceful response to Russia's state-run doping program, lobbying international sports officials for more aggressive sanctions and for an overhaul of the global regulatory system.

Executives at the nearby United States Olympic Committee's headquarters have a different agenda. They are lobbying the same officials to award the 2024 Summer Games to Los Angeles, a likely financial boon for the committee, and have pressured Congress not to amplify the antidoping concerns.

The competing agendas have put some of the most powerful sports executives in the world in conflict as the Olympic Committee enters the final months of its effort to bring the Games back to the United States for the first time since 2002.

"Fighting with an organization responsible for giving future Olympic Games — it's a big mistake," said Vitaly Smirnov, an influential Russian Olympic official.

He singled out criticisms by Travis Tygart, America's antidoping chief, who has argued for severe penalties against Russia. "This gentleman is doing a very counterproductive job with respect to the Los Angeles bid," Mr. Smirnov said.

The choice for the 2024 Games is down to Los Angeles and Paris, and United States Olympic officials and other powerful interests involved with the bid have expressed concern to members of Congress that the clean-sports crusade could alienate some of the global officials who will make the decision.

Mr. Tygart is to continue his crusade on Tuesday, when he is scheduled to address a House subcommittee about the doping scandal and the ways in which the global sports system could be improved.

Testifying alongside him will be Michael Phelps, the world's most decorated Olympian; Adam Nelson, an American shot putter who was awarded a gold medal nearly a decade after his 2004 Olympic performance when a competitor was disqualified for doping; as well as officials from the I.O.C. and the World Anti-Doping Agency, to which the United States contributes $2 million annually.

Scott Blackmun, chief executive of the United States Olympic Committee, acknowledged that over the last year his organization had discussed the pending bid, along with a range of other issues, with both the House and the Senate.

The Senate Commerce committee, which has not called a hearing but confirmed that its parallel inquiry was continuing, said on Saturday that it had "challenged suggestions that the 2024 bid is a legitimate rationale for stopping or delaying necessary oversight of doping in international competition."

Mr. Blackmun said he thought a congressional hearing would be "more productive" after international sports officials had signaled how they planned to address the scandal, and that he supported lawmakers' desire to stay informed. He also said he supported the fight for clean sports, but that his organization prefers a quieter approach.

As the Russian doping scandal was roiling global sports weeks ahead of the Rio Olympics, with sports officials scrambling to respond to the pressure Mr. Tygart and others were applying in calling for extreme sanctions, the American Olympic committee worked to stave off congressional attention.

"We were not saying hearings were inappropriate, but instead that right in front of the Olympic Games is not the right time," Mr. Blackmun said.

"Travis's style, I would be lying if I told you it wasn't having an impact," he said of Mr. Tygart and the nation's Olympic bid. "At the end of the day, he's doing his job, and he's doing it really well. Would we like him to be a little bit more of a silver-tongued devil? Yes, we would."

Mr. Tygart shrugged off the critiques of his methods. “It’s not unusual when you’re trying to do the right thing that there are attempts to pressure you to back off these fundamental values,” he said.

Though based mere miles apart, the two prominent officials rarely cross paths in person. If ever, it might happen at the airport, since each travels frequently. They speak by phone every two to three months.

While both organizations are aimed at serving American athletes, their pursuits are not always in harmony. The tension over the last year has not surprised American athletes who have expressed frustration at what they call global officials’ hesitancy to discipline Russia for systematic cheating.

“The I.O.C. is responsible for the integrity of the Olympics and keeping it functioning, and they’re not doing it,” said Sarah Konrad, an American biathlete who until last month was chairwoman of the United States Olympic Committee’s athlete advisory council. “I know Scott Blackmun thinks more needs to be done by WADA and the I.O.C., but he’s not willing to get out and stand on a pulpit and say that because of the bid.”

Asked to respond to Ms. Konrad’s statement, Mr. Blackmun called her “a very smart person.”

The host for the 2024 Games will be determined in September by secret ballots cast by the roughly 100 members of the International Olympic Committee, representing countries from Brazil to Liechtenstein to North Korea. Russia has three members.

The global officials are accustomed to autonomy and may bristle at this week’s scrutiny from the American government, prompting some like Ms. Konrad to wonder if a hearing could cause more harm than good.

“We want the I.O.C. to be independent, nothing to do with politics,” Gerhard Heiberg, a longtime I.O.C. member from Norway, said. “That is of course not possible, but it could be very difficult to have one nation getting involved in how we are handling doping and putting pressure on us.”

Mr. Heiberg said that whims often guided the individual votes of I.O.C. decision-makers. "On Sept. 13, when we choose between Los Angeles and Paris, a lot of people will vote with their hearts," he said.

Congress's interest in the doping scandal, Mr. Tygart's activism and the United States' inquiries into international sports corruption — from the FIFA case focused on soccer's global governing body to a Justice Department investigation into the Russian doping scandal — could inform how some of his colleagues voted, he said.

"It could affect some members — 'you want the Games, fine, but don't mix things up,' " Mr. Heiberg said.

Gian-Franco Kasper of Switzerland, who sits on the I.O.C.'s executive board, also said that Mr. Tygart's outspokenness, coupled with Donald J. Trump's election, could diminish Los Angeles's attractiveness as host.

Mr. Trump has expressed public support for the Olympic bid, though some of his policies — most notably on immigration, including his recent executive order barring visitors from seven predominantly Muslim nations — have caused concern among sports officials.

Mr. Blackmun said the American Olympic committee had received assurances from the State Department and Homeland Security that global athletes and officials would have no trouble entering the United States in 2024.

"The Games are more than seven years away at this point and, candidly, the I.O.C. has been through this a number of times," Mr. Blackmun said. "I think they have the ability to look past what I would call the short-term political or situational environment."

As a dwindling number of cities have expressed willingness to host the Olympics, the I.O.C.'s president has suggested he would like to see fewer "losers" in the bid process, setting off recent speculation that both Paris and Los Angeles could be chosen at the same time to host two future Summer Olympics, for 2024 and 2028.

Even so, Mr. Blackmun emphasized last week in his fifth-floor office in downtown Colorado Springs, decorated with oversize photographs of American athletes marching in various opening ceremonies, that the United States was exclusively focused on hosting in 2024. If Los Angeles receives the bid, Mr. Blackmun said, the Summer Games could make an example of the country's strong antidoping system.

A 10-minute drive north, Mr. Tygart walked into the antidoping agency's staff kitchen and pointed to an array of motivational words decorating the wall. "Courage," he said, gesturing above the refrigerator. "That's the most important one."

Mr. Tygart's colleague Edwin Moses — an Olympic medalist and chairman of the American antidoping agency's board — expressed consternation that the agency's principled positions might undermine the bid.

"If standing up for the rights of athletes and fair play somehow makes a country less likely to host the Olympic Games — wow," he said. "That says about all you need to know about that process. It's also exactly why sport has no business trying to police itself."

Ms. Konrad, the Olympic biathlete, said she appreciated that Mr. Tygart had sacrificed a cozy relationship with Olympic officials, displaying the independence he and others have called for regulators to embrace at the global level.

"I can sympathize with people showing restraint because they want L.A. to happen," Ms. Konrad said. "But a clean playing field is more important to me than a home playing field."

At the Heart of a Vast Doping Network, an Alias

BY MICHAEL POWELL | MARCH 26, 2018

ON AUG. 25, 2015, a Swiss postal inspector reached into the river of 300,000 parcels that pour into that nation every day and, for a routine inspection, plucked out two packages arriving from Arizona. Inspectors unwrapped them and found serried rows of bottles.

The bottles were suspected of containing performance-enhancing drugs, so they were shipped to an antidoping laboratory for testing. Chemists discovered three synthetic compounds that are illicit gold for cheating athletes. One sped the healing of tendons and ligaments. Another helped build muscle mass. A third stimulated the body to burn fat.

The Swiss authorities notified the organization in the United States that investigates sports doping, the United States Anti-Doping Agency, and shared the return-address sticker. The packages were shipped by someone named Thomas Mann.

His name drew puzzled shrugs from Usada investigators. That name had never crossed their radar, and they could not find a home listing for someone with that name in their database in Arizona or anywhere else.

The name was then stored in the organization's computer system and largely forgotten, until it resurfaced in a different context several months later, triggering an intense pursuit of Thomas Mann and an aggressive investigation of his enterprise that involved federal law enforcement as well as antidoping officials.

The existence of the investigation and its extraordinary findings have not been previously reported.

Investigators believe what they uncovered was a trafficker who sat at the center of one of the broadest sports doping networks in American history, with tendrils that extended to Europe and Asia.

In one year, he shipped parcels containing performance-enhancing drugs to more than 8,000 people, they determined. His substance of choice was peptides, a newly popular (though banned) substance among athletes that is essentially a building block for protein.

His clientele included a dozen pro football players and coaches; pro baseball players and a major league batting coach; and top track and field athletes. There were Olympians and potential Olympians, from discus throwers to sprinters to pole-vaulters to weight lifters to wrestlers.

Investigators assembled what they considered a hay pile of incriminating evidence: surveillance video of the man making the shipments; invoices and payment receipts; email messages; and testimony from several athletes who purchased drugs from him that corroborated the nature of his business.

Yet the dealer has not faced criminal charges. He distributed drugs that inhabit a hazy gray zone. Prosecutors generally treat the possession of peptides, which are illegal without a medical prescription, as a misdemeanor.

Investigators also determined something else: The man's name was not Thomas Mann. His real name was Michael A. Moorcones, and he had left the faintest of footprints. Born in Virginia, he was a lawyer with no law office, a distributor of sports drugs with no formal training as a pharmacist.

I set out to find Moorcones. I drove 30 miles south of Phoenix to Queen Creek, Ariz., where suburbs expire in sun-blasted desert and the Superstition Mountains rise gray and jagged. I rang a doorbell in a subdivision. A balding, middle-aged man opened the door.

Michael Moorcones?

He nodded. "Yes?"

I'm a reporter, I told him, and athletes tell me they purchased your performance-enhancing drugs. They say your substances help them out-train and outperform athletes who compete clean.

Can we talk?

ADAM SIMPSON

Moorcones offered a hint of a chuckle. "I wouldn't be interested in ever talking to anybody about anything. O.K.?"

He moved to close the door.

THE BUSINESS

In late December 2015, about four months after the Swiss authorities had flagged the shipments from Thomas Mann, Al Jazeera released an explosive documentary called "The Dark Side: Secrets of the Sports Dopers." A retired professional hurdler from Britain had worked with the news organization to penetrate the world of illicit sports doping while carrying a hidden camera.

An intriguing name was tucked into the Al Jazeera documentary. Underground chemists spoke with reverence of a Svengali who produced and sold them high-quality sports drugs. His name was Thomas Mann.

A chemist explained in the documentary how fastidious he had to be when ordering performance-enhancing drugs from Mann: "If you even use the wrong language with him, saying, 'Oh, I'm going to use this,' right away, boom, you'd be kicked off."

Investigators pulled at Thomas Mann's internet veil and found that he was using an alias, a name perhaps borrowed from the famous German novelist. He called his business Authentiquevie (French for "authentic life"); another forum, DatBTrue, provided a menu of his peptides and hormones, accompanied by detailed explanations of each drug. Four-star customer testimonials piled up.

"Tom carries it and is the only guy I trust to deliver actual peptides and not useless vials," read one.

His business model, according to investigators, was clever. They believe he operated the DatBTrue forum, a go-to place for savvy discussion of peptides. When an athlete on the forum would inquire about obtaining peptides, Moorcones, using a different name, would steer the athlete to Thomas Mann. So he was sending potential customers to himself.

Moorcones, in the guise of Thomas Mann, or Tom Mann, would then rigorously vet the customers to make sure they were who they claimed to be and would be trustworthy clients.

In the one year that Moorcones was under investigation, he had $1 million in sales.

Moorcones's business was a raging river in a much larger doping ecosystem. The demand for performance-enhancing drugs extends to every corner of professional and amateur sports, and well beyond. Name any sport, and chances are good that someone playing it has been caught doping in the past few months.

Then there are wealthy users who flock to anti-aging medical clinics in search of youthful elixirs. They find doctors who will prescribe peptides and human growth hormone. The patients take all of these in hopes of adding muscle mass, smoothing wrinkles and reclaiming body definition and sexual vitality.

Moorcones served both ends of this market, from athletes to the aging. All came to his online forum in search of the latest wonder drug.

Moorcones purported that his products were intended for lab use only. In a 2014 email, he wrote: "I have the following batches available for in vitro purposes only. Peptides: Modified GRF (1-29) (2mg) @ $35/vial; $31/10 vials." But a cursory reading of his customers' online comments indicated that they were not being used that way.

Dr. Todd B. Nippoldt, an endocrinologist at the Mayo Clinic in Rochester, Minn., spoke to the scientific and health consequences of unregulated and illegal use.

"These people are carrying out quite sophisticated experiments on themselves at doses that far exceed anything in a lab," Nippoldt said. "It's quite remarkable and dangerous."

EMERGENCE OF PEPTIDES

The original wonder drug of sports doping was steroids, and it remains the gold standard for athletic cheaters. There is nothing, doctors and athletes say, quite like the muscle-firing boost provided by synthetic testosterone.

Steroid use peaked in the 1980s and 1990s, and records set during that era were Popeye-like. Olympic records usually fall every few Games; some records set during the steroid era have stood untouched for decades. This is no less true of Major League Baseball, where swollen sluggers made a mockery of the record books in recent decades.

Then testing for steroids improved and some sports toughened their rules against doping. Steroids became a riskier play. But that did not stop cheating. Block one back alley, and sophisticated chemists scurry down another. The aim, always, is to find ways to build muscle mass, burn fat, aid recovery and increase the ability of the body to expand its aerobic capacity. This underground world soon turned its eyes toward human growth hormones and peptides, strings of amino acids and the building blocks of proteins.

Some peptides trigger reactions in the body similar to those of anabolic steroids. Others, known as secretagogues, stimulate the human pituitary gland to release excess growth hormone. A well-regarded scientific study in Australia found that growth hormone helped sprinters improve their times by 4 percent. As a typical 100-meter race is won or lost by hundredths of a second, a 4 percent improvement would represent a considerable advantage.

The Al Jazeera documentary underlined that peptides had become a prime ingredient in a cheater's performance cocktail. The documentary caught Taylor Teagarden, a major league catcher, saying on hidden camera that he had taken peptides and never been caught. (Major League Baseball remedied that oversight and suspended Teagarden for 80 games a few months after the documentary was released.)

Dr. Robert Salvatori, an expert on growth hormone at Johns Hopkins, noted that athletes were quite shrewd about the effects that drugs have on their bodies. History demonstrates that they often recognize the performance-boosting power before the medical community does.

"It took scientists until 1996 to prove the muscle-boosting powers of steroids — which athletes knew years earlier," he said. "We are running way behind."

Seeking to learn more about the latest tactics in sports doping, I went to Phoenix to meet with Cody Bidlow, a former professional sprinter and personal coach. A year ago, the United States Anti-Doping Agency discovered that Bidlow had ordered peptides from Moorcones's website. He received a four-year suspension.

A lean and muscular fellow, Bidlow described for me how he came to use peptides. He had been a sprinter at Grand Canyon University in 2015 when he sustained a hamstring injury. He was no potential Olympian. He simply wanted to run a few more races, so he asked around at elite gyms for a quick doping fix.

“I had always been around people who used peptides and H.G.H.,” he said, although he declined to name names. “It sounded like peptides are super-effective.”

He wrote down the names of suppliers. He found a lot of fast talkers who excited no trust. (The head of Switzerland’s antidoping organization told me that his agency’s tests have shown that 80 percent of the peptides advertised on the web are adulterated or outright fakes.)

Then Bidlow learned of Thomas Mann’s site, which was refreshingly professional. And Mann’s peptides were real. “This wasn’t ‘bro science’; he is a pure brainiac,” Bidlow said. “He would post scientific studies breaking down how a peptide worked.”

We sat in a coffee shop as Bidlow gave me a tutorial on peptides. He described which worked, which were difficult to detect and which were not worth the trouble. He said coaches and athletes — particularly sprinters — were enamored of something called insulin-like growth factor-1, known as IGF-1. It promotes healing and builds muscle in a fashion similar to anabolic steroids. IGF-1 occurs naturally in the body, and antidoping tests struggle to distinguish the natural from the synthetic.

No sprinter or baseball player has ever tested positive for IGF-1. Do not take that to mean no sprinter or baseball player has ever used it; they just haven’t been caught.

The antidoping world has occasional successes. In 2015 and 2016, Dodgers pitcher Josh Ravin, Indians outfielder Marlon Byrd and Braves pitcher Andrew McKirahan tested positive for peptides. Major League Baseball suspended all of them.

But the case of the retired baseball star Alex Rodriguez is more typical. Anthony Bosch, who said he supplied Rodriguez with drugs, told “60 Minutes” that his witch’s brew included peptides. Rodriguez was suspended by baseball, but not because he failed a drug test. The league connected him to doping through an investigation it started only after a news report broke the story of Bosch’s company, Biogenesis.

'NO LEGAL FOOTHOLD'

Faced with the limits of testing technology, antidoping officials and investigators have asked the Food and Drug Administration and Congress to tighten laws and crack down on peptides and growth hormone.

For Drug Enforcement Administration officials, the problem lies with the weak wording of the laws that currently govern peptides.

"If I catch you with heroin, it's a controlled substance and illegal — that's easy," said Douglas W. Coleman, the special agent in charge of the D.E.A.'s Phoenix Division. "If I find human growth hormone, I have to build a case to show that it's significantly outside what it can be prescribed for.

"Peptides are more difficult still. There's really no legal foothold."

The F.D.A. holds clearer regulatory authority; its officials could write tougher regulatory language and crack down on peptides and growth hormone. But agency investigators have paid scant attention to this black market. I asked, repeatedly and over many weeks, to speak with an F.D.A. official about the regulation of peptides and growth hormone.

In the end, an agency spokeswoman sent a boilerplate email.

"The F.D.A. takes seriously its mission to protect the health of the American public," wrote the spokeswoman, Theresa Eisenman. "There are many complex factors involved in how cases involving the sale or distribution of illegal products are investigated and ultimately prosecuted."

Her email cited three successful peptide prosecutions involving four people during the past three years. Each of the offenders received a light punishment.

Seeking a more detailed explanation, I called a former top F.D.A. official. He spoke on condition of anonymity, as he remains involved with these issues in the private sector. He described the F.D.A.'s stance as defensible. It has a small staff of about 200 agents, and they focus on plagues like tainted and counterfeit drugs, which endanger thousands of unsuspecting customers. The societal impact of peptides and growth hormone is far less severe, clearly.

The former official described the world of illicit peptide and hormones as caveat emptor — buyer beware. "If rich patients and athletes are going to anti-aging clinics or the web in search of unregistered drugs, they know the risk," he said.

The decision to downgrade prosecutions has all but decriminalized the mass distribution and use of powerful and untested drugs for athletes.

THE ATHLETES

Investigators discovered that Moorcones was shipping his products from a U.P.S. store wedged between a supermarket and real estate office on the suburban frontier of Queen Creek. Video surveillance revealed that Moorcones's septuagenarian parents often went with him to mail his parcels.

Eventually investigators obtained Moorcones's customer list of more than 8,000 names. It was a rich hunting ground. Investigators found the names of pro athletes and forwarded the information to their leagues.

Major League Baseball ended up suspending two minor leaguers. The National Football League was another matter. The Al Jazeera documentary had named six players as likely dopers, and the N.F.L. penalized not a single one. The Moorcones investigation yielded more names, which were shared with the league. The N.F.L. has penalized none of the players.

Track and field athletes, weight lifters and wrestlers are another matter. The United States Anti-Doping Agency has jurisdiction over these sports and can punish athletes who violate doping protocols.

Usada handed down a raft of penalties to Moorcones's customers. Jason Young, a 35-year-old discus thrower and coach from Lubbock, Tex., who competed in the 2012 Summer Olympics, was suspended, as was Nick Mossberg, a pole-vaulter who competed at the 2012 United States Olympic trials and planned to try again in

2016. The investigation also netted a wrestler from Colorado and a weight lifter who graduated from M.I.T.

All acknowledged ordering peptides from Tom Mann. None of these athletes had tested positive.

Bidlow and Mossberg, the pole-vaulter, had worked and trained at Altis, an elite athletic training campus in Phoenix. Numerous Olympic athletes train there under the tutelage of coaches with global reputations.

I called the recruiting director at Altis, Andreas Behm, who also coaches the sprinters and hurdlers. Bidlow and Mossberg, he said, had simply "gone rogue." The elite training center, he insisted, had no larger problem with doping.

'LOSING A TRUE HERO'

The investigation of Moorcones stalled last year. The United States attorney in Phoenix had taken a hard look and given up because a federal agency — the F.D.A. or the D.E.A. — was not willing to bring a case. His distribution of peptides, they apparently decided, was not worth prosecuting. A lawyer for Moorcones demanded immunity for his client.

Moorcones shut down his website and claimed online that he was ill. Worried customers speculated that his own drugs had sickened him. "I feel for the guy," one customer wrote. "The community of illegal experimental medicine is losing a true hero."

Other clients speculated correctly that Mann was under investigation; they began to worry that their names had fallen into the hands of law enforcement. They were correct.

Moorcones politely bid everyone goodbye. "I've enjoyed serving everyone through the years," he wrote on his Authentiquevie site.

Within months, investigators noticed that one of Moorcones's prominent, high-volume customers had taken his business to a dealer in Florida, where anti-aging clinics peddling peptides and hormones grow like sugar cane. Other clients turned to an oft-investigated but still active peptide trafficker in Louisiana.

There was still much investigators did not understand about Moorcones's operation. He distributed such massive volumes of illicit substances, but they were never able to determine the source of the drugs. Was he purchasing them from somewhere and reselling to athletes, or was he somehow manufacturing them himself? And were his parents aware of what they were shipping?

Back on the edge of the desert in Arizona, I persuaded Moorcones to keep the door open another minute or two. "People all have their own agenda," he told me.

I allowed that this might be true. Any story grows more complicated when you hear both sides, I said. Why not tell me yours?

He smiled faintly. "I wouldn't be the person to give it to you anyway. Thank you."

This time, Moorcones shut the door.

A Better Body in a Pill? Experts Urge Caution on SARMs

BY ANAHAD O'CONNOR | APRIL 12, 2018

MANY ATHLETES AND GYM-GOERS are turning to a popular but potentially dangerous new pill to help them build muscle and gain strength: a steroid alternative known as SARMs.

The pills are widely marketed online as "legal steroids" that provide the muscle-building benefits of anabolic steroids without the troubling side effects. And while the products are legal — at least so far — their spread has alarmed health authorities, who say they are not necessarily safe.

Drug companies developed SARMs, which stands for selective androgen receptor modulators, as an alternative to anabolic steroids for people who suffer from age and disease-related muscle loss. But they are the subject of ongoing clinical trials and have not been approved for use by the Food and Drug Administration.

In October, the agency issued a public advisory cautioning that SARMs were unapproved drugs linked to "serious safety concerns," including the potential for an increased risk of liver toxicity, heart attacks and strokes.

A month later, a study published in JAMA revealed that products marketed as SARMs were frequently misbranded and tainted with unlisted ingredients. Out of 44 products that were purchased online and analyzed, only about half contained an actual SARM, while 10 percent contained none at all. Roughly 40 percent had other hormones and unapproved drugs. Several contained a drug that was abandoned by GlaxoSmithKline a decade ago after it was found to cause cancer in animals.

The long-term consequences of using SARMs are largely unknown, and people who purchase products marketed as them cannot be entirely sure what they are putting in their bodies, said Dr. Shalender

Bhasin, the director of research programs in men's health, aging and metabolism at Brigham and Women's Hospital and an author of the JAMA report.

"We don't know whether these compounds are safe," he said, "but we do know that some of them have side effects."

That has not stopped many people from experimenting with them.

Thaddeus Owen, 42, a self-described biohacker who lives in Saint Paul, Minn., began using SARMs in 2016 in combination with a diet and exercise program. He said that the pills helped him pack on five pounds of muscle in four weeks, which he documented on his website, "PrimalHacker." He argued that informed adults should be allowed "to experiment on ourselves and improve our biology," but added, "this is definitely a use-at-your-own-risk type of supplement."

Anti-doping officials have known about SARMs for some time and have seen an increasing number of elite athletes using them. Since 2015, the United States Anti-Doping Agency has imposed sanctions on more than two dozen track and field stars, weight lifters, cyclists, mixed martial artists and others for testing positive for a variety of SARMs, most frequently one called ostarine.

Last year, Joakim Noah, a center for the New York Knicks, was suspended for 20 games for testing positive for a SARM. The college basketball star Allonzo Trier of the Arizona Wildcats was also suspended for using SARMs. And in October, a top CrossFit Games competitor, Ricky Garard, was stripped of his third-place title after testing positive for two SARMs: ostarine and testolone.

While the underground use of SARMs has made them controversial, the drugs could one day serve a crucial purpose for many patients.

Scientists developed SARMs decades ago to counter the age-related decline in muscle and strength that tends to begin around middle age and that can contribute to falls and broken bones. Many chronic diseases, such as cancer, heart failure and kidney disease, are also punctuated by a loss of muscle and physical mobility.

Anabolic and androgenic steroids such as testosterone can help people regain muscle and physical function. But they act on many tissues throughout the body and have been tied to a litany of potential side effects, including prostate problems and cardiovascular events.

SARMs were designed to selectively target skeletal muscle and spare other tissues, in an attempt to reduce some of these unwanted side effects. A number of trials are looking at their usefulness in cancer patients, people recovering from hip surgery, and postmenopausal women with urinary incontinence linked to weak pelvic muscles.

A three-week trial at Boston University demonstrated that LGD-4033, a SARM developed by Ligand Pharmaceuticals, was safe and tolerable in healthy men, producing "significant gains in muscle mass and strength" without raising levels of a protein linked to prostate cancer. But it had other effects as well, for instance causing a drop in HDL cholesterol, the protective kind, which raised questions about its effects on heart health.

"Long-term studies are needed to clarify the effects of long-term SARM administration on cardiovascular risk," the authors concluded.

Thomas O'Connor, a doctor who founded a men's health clinic and wrote a book called "America on Steroids," said that many of his patients are anabolic steroid users who turned to SARMs because they were told that they were safe and nontoxic. He said that since 2010 he has seen "hundreds, maybe over 1,000 men on SARMs" from all walks of life: police officers, defense workers, amateur athletes, accountants and others.

It's hard to determine the precise impact of SARMs because many people who use them combine them with other drugs, supplements and substances, Dr. O'Connor said. But one thing he often sees among people using SARMs is that their cholesterol profiles worsen and their liver enzymes rise, a sign of increased strain on their livers. Some also experience diminished sex drive, hair loss, acne and irritability, though it's often difficult to know whether it's the SARMs causing these symptoms or some other unlisted ingredients in the products.

As a longtime power lifter, Dr. O'Connor said he relates to a lot of his patients and understands their desire to be bigger, stronger and fitter. But he counsels them to give up the drugs they are using because they are jeopardizing their health.

"I always tell them the same thing," he said. "These are illicit agents. They're not supported by expert guidelines and they're dangerous. So don't take them."

The Council for Responsible Nutrition, a supplement industry trade group, launched a campaign on social media, #SARMSCanHarm, and is working with sports clubs, fitness groups and coaches around the country. The military and federal government also have an awareness campaign about risky products called Operation Supplement Safety.

Patricia Deuster, a professor of military and emergency medicine at the Uniformed Services University of the Health Sciences, said SARMs are popular among some soldiers because they are easier to access than anabolic steroids, but she warns them there are hazards, citing one soldier who suffered liver damage and could not deploy with his unit because he was hospitalized after using a product containing SARMs and other ingredients.

"We try to tell them that there are other ways that they can achieve their goals without risking their health or their ability to maintain their deployment status," Dr. Deuster said. "We are trying to educate them."

U.S. Lawmakers Seek to Criminalize Doping in Global Competitions

BY REBECCA R. RUIZ | JUNE 12, 2018

UNITED STATES LAWMAKERS took a step on Tuesday toward criminalizing doping in international sports, introducing a bill in the House that would attach prison time to the use, manufacturing or distribution of performance-enhancing drugs in global competitions.

The legislation, inspired by the Russian doping scandal, would echo the Foreign Corrupt Practices Act, which makes it illegal to bribe foreign officials to gain a business advantage. The statute would be the first of its kind with global reach, empowering American prosecutors to act on doping violations abroad, and to file fraud charges of a different variety than those the Justice Department brought against top international soccer officials in 2015.

Although American leagues like Major League Baseball would not be affected by the legislation, which would apply only to competitions among countries, it could apply to a league's athletes when they participate in global events like the Ryder Cup, the Davis Cup or the World Baseball Classic.

The law would establish America's jurisdiction over international sports events, even those outside of the United States, if they include at least three other nations, with at least four American athletes participating or two American companies acting as sponsors. It would also enhance the ability of cheated athletes and corporate sponsors to seek damages, expanding the window of time during which civil lawsuits could be filed.

To justify the United States' broader jurisdiction over global competitions, the House bill invokes the United States' contribution to the World Anti-Doping Agency, the global regulator of drugs in sports. At $2.3 million, the United States' annual contribution is the single largest of any nation. "Doping fraud in major international competitions also effectively defrauds the United States," the bill states.

EMILY BERL FOR THE NEW YORK TIMES

Grigory Rodchenkov, who ran the Sochi laboratory, said he developed a three-drug cocktail of banned substances that he provided to dozens of Russian athletes.

The lawmakers behind the bill were instrumental in the creation of the 2012 Magnitsky Act, which gave the government the right to freeze financial assets and impose visa restrictions on Russian nationals accused of serious human rights violations and corruption. On Tuesday, the lawmakers framed their interest in sports fraud around international relations and broader networks of crime that can accompany cheating.

"Doping fraud is a crime in which big money, state assets and transnational criminals gain advantage and honest athletes and companies are defrauded," said Sheila Jackson Lee, Democrat of Texas, who introduced the legislation on Tuesday. "This practice, some of it state-sanctioned, has the ability to undermine international relations, and is often connected to more nefarious actions by state actors."

Along with Ms. Jackson Lee, the bill was sponsored by two other congressional representatives, Michael C. Burgess, Republican of Texas, and Gwen Moore, Democrat of Wisconsin.

It was put forward just as Russia prepares to host soccer's World Cup, which starts Thursday. That sporting event will be the nation's biggest since the 2014 Sochi Olympics, where one of the most elaborate doping ploys in history took place.

The bill, the Rodchenkov Anti-Doping Act, takes its name from Dr. Grigory Rodchenkov, the chemist who ran Russia's antidoping laboratory for 10 years before he spoke out about the state-sponsored cheating he had helped carry out — most notoriously in Sochi. At those Games, Dr. Rodchenkov said, he concealed widespread drug use among Russia's top Olympians by tampering with more than 100 urine samples with the help of Russia's Federal Security Service.

Investigations commissioned by international sports regulators confirmed his account and concluded that Russia had cheated across competitions and years, tainting the performance of more than 1,000 athletes. In early 2017, American intelligence officials concluded that Russia's meddling in the 2016 American election had been, in part, a form of retribution for the Olympic doping scandal, whose disclosures Russian officials blamed on the United States.

Nations including Germany, France, Italy, Kenya and Spain have established criminal penalties for sports doping perpetrated within their borders. Russia, too, passed a law in 2017 that made it a crime to assist or coerce doping, though no known charges have been brought under that law to date.

Under the proposed American law, criminal penalties for offenders would include a prison term of up to five years as well as fines that could stretch to $250,000 for individuals and $1 million for organizations.

"We could have real change if people think they could actually go to jail for this," said Jim Walden, a lawyer for Dr. Rodchenkov, who met with the lawmakers as they considered the issue in recent months. "I think it will have a meaningful impact on coaches and athletes if they realize they might not be able to travel outside of their country for fear of being arrested."

The legislation also authorizes civil actions for doping fraud, giving athletes who may have been cheated in competitions — as well as corporations acting as sponsors — the right to sue in federal court to recover damages from people who may have defrauded competitions.

Ms. Jackson Lee cited the American runner Alysia Montaño, who placed fifth in the 800 meters at the 2012 Summer Olympics. Two Russian women who placed first and third in that race were later disqualified for doping, elevating Ms. Montaño years later. "She had rightfully finished third, which would have earned her a bronze medal," Ms. Jackson Lee said, noting the financial benefits and sponsorships Ms. Montaño could have captured.

The bill would establish a window of seven years for criminal actions and 10 years for civil lawsuits. It also seeks to protect whistleblowers from retaliation, making it illegal to take "adverse action" against a person because he or she has disclosed information about doping fraud.

Dr. Rodchenkov, who has lived in the United States since fall 2015, has been criminally charged in Russia after he publicly deconstructed the cheating he said he carried out on orders from a state minister.

"While he was complicit in Russia's past bad acts, Dr. Rodchenkov regrets his past role in Russia's state-run doping program and seeks to atone for it by aiding the effort to clean up international sports and to curb the corruption rampant in Russia," Ms. Jackson Lee said, calling Tuesday's bill "an important step to stemming the tide of Russian corruption in sport and restoring confidence in international competition."

Glossary

adverse To go against or cause harm.

allegation A statement that is not yet proven.

anabolic steroid A man-made steroid hormone similar to testosterone that promotes muscle growth.

anodyne Medicine that kills pain.

arbitration The act of settling a dispute through a third party.

biological passport A tool designed to discourage doping by measuring attributes of an athlete's blood over time to detect abnormal readings.

blood doping To withdraw some of an athlete's blood and return it to the body at a later date in order to aid athletic performance.

capitalism An economic system in which resources and production are owned privately and distributed by competition in a free market.

censure To make an official statement of disapproval.

dissident A person who disagrees with a group.

doping The act of administering drugs that will cause a sporting performance to improve or decline.

endorsement An arrangement in which a company provides payments to an athlete in order for that athlete to advertise their products or services.

euphemism The substitution of a mild term for one that is too strong or unpleasant.

forensic Belonging to or used in courts of law.

hemoglobin A protein in red blood cells that transports oxygen in a vertebrate's body.

indictment An official document that charges a person with a crime.

methodology A system of methods used in a certain activity.

pharmacology The study of drugs' makeup and effects in medicine.

physiology The activities and life process of a living creature.

procure To obtain.

quixotic Something that is impractical or foolish.

saline solution A mixture of salt water that is the same composition of the human body.

skeleton competition A race that involves a person riding a sled head-first down a dangerous ice track.

socialism A system by which a society's government owns and administers the means of production and distribution of goods.

steroid Various chemical mixtures including hormones.

subpoena A written order commanding a person to appear in court.

testosterone A male hormone that causes the development of the reproductive system and secondary sex characteristics such as improved strength.

therapeutic use exemption Permission to use certain banned drugs for athletes who need them for medical conditions such as asthma.

treble damages Three times the amount of actual damages awarded to a plaintiff in a court case.

World Anti-Doping Agency (WADA) An official organization that regulates the use of drugs in sports.

Media Literacy Terms

"Media literacy" refers to the ability to access, understand, critically assess and create media. The following terms are important components of media literacy, and they will help you critically engage with the articles in this title.

angle The aspect of a news story that a journalist focuses on and develops.

attribution The method by which a source is identified or by which facts and information are assigned to the person who provided them.

balance Principle of journalism that both perspectives of an argument should be presented in a fair way.

bias A disposition of prejudice in favor of a certain idea, person or perspective.

byline Name of the writer, usually placed between the headline and the story.

chronological order Method of writing a story presenting the details of the story in the order in which they occurred.

column A type of story that is a regular feature, often on a recurring topic, written by the same journalist, generally known as a columnist.

commentary A type of story that is an expression of opinion on recent events by a journalist generally known as a commentator.

credibility The quality of being trustworthy and believable, said of a journalistic source.

critical review A type of story that describes an event or work of art, such as a theater performance, film, concert, book, restaurant, radio or television program, exhibition or musical piece and offers critical assessment of its quality and reception.

editorial Article of opinion or interpretation.

feature story Article designed to entertain as well as to inform

human interest story A type of story that focuses on individuals and how events or issues affect their life, generally offering a sense of relatability to the reader.

impartiality Principle of journalism that a story should not reflect a journalist's bias and should contain balance.

intention The motive or reason behind something, such as the publication of a news story.

interview story A type of story in which the facts are gathered primarily by interviewing another person or persons.

motive The reason behind something, such as the publication of a news story or a source's perspective on an issue.

news story An article or style of expository writing that reports news, generally in a straightforward fashion and without editorial comment.

op-ed An opinion piece that reflects a prominent individual's opinion on a topic of interest.

paraphrase The summary of an individual's words, with attribution, rather than a direct quotation of the person's exact words.

plagiarism An attempt to pass another person's work as one's own without attribution.

reliability The quality of being dependable and accurate, said of a journalistic source.

sports reporting A type of story that reports on sporting events or topics related to sports.

tone A manner of expression in writing or speech.

Media Literacy Questions

1. Identify the various sources cited in the article "Doping Tests Urged for All Harness Horses Before Races at State Tracks" (on page 14). How does Deane McGowen attribute information to each of these sources in his article? How effective are McGowen's attributions in helping the reader identify his sources?

2. In "Use of Drugs at Olympics Found to Be Widespread" (on page 17), journalist Neil Amdur directly quotes Dr. David James. What are the strengths of the use of a direct quote as opposed to a paraphrase? What are the weaknesses?

3. Compare the headlines of "Strike Keeps Tour de France Riders on Pills and Needles" (on page 25) and "I.O.C. Issues Doping Report" (on page 42). Which is a more compelling headline, and why? How could the less compelling headline be changed to better draw the reader's interest?

4. What type of story is "Gary Wadler, Antidoping Pioneer, Had a Gift for Straight Talk" (on page 47)? Can you identify another article in this collection that is the same type of story?

5. Does Michael Janofsky demonstrate the journalistic principle of impartiality in his article "Citing Drug Use, Olympic Official Proposes a Ban on Weight Lifting" (on page 54)? If so, how did he do so? If not, what could he have included to make his article more impartial?

6. Does "Drugs Pervade Sport in Russia, World Anti-Doping Agency Report Finds" (on page 63) use multiple sources? What are the strengths of using multiple sources in a journalistic piece? What are the weaknesses of relying heavily on only one source or a few sources?

7. "Armstrong's Wall of Silence Fell Rider by Rider" (on page 94) features photographs. What do the photographs add to the article?

8. "Enough. Give Russia Its Flag Back, Then Make Real Changes." (on page 180) is an example of a critical review. What is the purpose of a critical review? Do you feel this article achieved that purpose?

9. "For Armstrong, a Confession Without Explanation" (on page 104) is an example of an interview. What are the benefits of providing readers with direct quotes of an interviewed subject's speech? Is the subject of an interview always a reliable source?

10. What is the intention of the article "The Home Run Explosion Is Not Exactly Beyond Suspicion" (on page 126)? How effectively does it achieve its intended purpose?

11. Analyze the authors' reporting in "Dog Doping at the Iditarod: Dallas Seavey, a Legend in the Sport, Is Named" (on page 136) and "Iditarod Doping Mystery: Who Slipped Tramadol to the Dogs" (on page 140). Do you think one journalist is more balanced in his reporting than the other? If so, why do you think so?

12. Often, as a news story develops, a journalist's attitude toward a subject may change. Compare "Antidoping Officials Get an Earful from Congress: 'What a Broken System' " (on page 173) and "U.S. Lawmakers Seek to Criminalize Doping in Global Competitions" (on page 204), both by Rebecca R. Ruiz. Did new information discovered between the publication of these two articles change Ruiz's perspective?

13. "Russian Insider Says State-Run Doping Fueled Olympic Gold" (on page 68) is an example of an interview. Can you identify skills or techniques used by Rebecca R. Ruiz and Michael Schwirtz to gather information from Grigory Rodchenkov?

14. Identify each of the sources in "At the Heart of a Vast Doping Network, an Alias" (on page 189) as a primary source or a secondary source. Evaluate the reliability and credibility of each source. How does your evaluation of each source change your perspective on this article?

Citations

All citations in this list are formatted according to the Modern Language Association's (MLA) style guide.

BOOK CITATION

NEW YORK TIMES EDITORIAL STAFF, THE. *Doping: The Sports World in Crisis.* New York: New York Times Educational Publishing, 2019.

ONLINE ARTICLE CITATIONS

AMDUR, NEIL. "Study May Renew 'Blood Doping' Debate." *The New York Times*, 4 May 1980, timesmachine.nytimes.com/timesmachine/1980/05/04/111237958.pdf.

AMDUR, NEIL. "Use of Drugs at Olympics Found to Be Widespread." *The New York Times*, 10 Nov. 1972, www.nytimes.com/1972/11/10/archives/use-of-drugs-at-olympics-found-to-be-widespread-drugging-at-games.html.

BRANCH, JOHN. "Iditarod Doping Mystery: Who Slipped Tramadol to the Dogs?" *The New York Times*, 24 Oct. 2017, www.nytimes.com/2017/10/24/sports/iditarod-doping-dallas-seavey.html.

CADY, STEVE. "Outcry on Wider Use of Drugs for Race Horses." *The New York Times*, 29 Mar. 1977, www.nytimes.com/1977/03/29/archives/issue-and-debate-outcry-on-wider-use-of-drugs-for-race-horses.html.

COHEN, ROGER. "In German Courthouse: Pain, Doping, Medals." *The New York Times*, 11 May 2000, www.nytimes.com/2000/05/11/sports/olympics-in-german-courthouse-pain-doping-medals.html.

CROUSE, KAREN. "For Olympic Hopefuls, Antidoping Rules Will Be an Adjustment." *The New York Times*, 25 Jan. 2015, www.nytimes.com/2015/01/26/sports/golf/for-olympic-hopefuls-antidoping-rules-will-be-an-adjustment.html.

CROUSE, KAREN. "For Tennis Players, Numbers in Antidoping Program Don't

Add Up." *The New York Times*, 3 July 2018, www.nytimes.com/2018/07/03/sports/tennis-doping.html.

HESS, JOHN L. "Strike Keeps Tour De France Riders on Pills and Needles." *The New York Times*, 10 July 1966, timesmachine.nytimes.com/timesmachine/1966/07/10/82481510.pdf.

HESS, JOHN L. "Turf Authorities Are Accused of 'Silence' Plot in Drugging." *The New York Times*, 20 Feb. 1966, timesmachine.nytimes.com/timesmachine/1966/02/20/121711610.pdf.

HOFFMAN, BENJAMIN. "Dog Doping at the Iditarod: Dallas Seavey, a Legend in the Sport, Is Named." *The New York Times*, 24 Oct. 2017, www.nytimes.com/2017/10/23/sports/iditarod-dog-doping-dallas-seavey.html.

JANOFSKY, MICHAEL. "Citing Drug Use, Olympic Official Proposes a Ban on Weight Lifting." *The New York Times*, 30 Sept. 1988, www.nytimes.com/1988/09/30/sports/citing-drug-use-olympic-official-proposes-a-ban-on-weight-lifting.html.

JANOFSKY, MICHAEL. "Johnson Loses Gold to Lewis After Drug Test." *The New York Times*, 27 Sept. 1988, www.nytimes.com/1988/09/27/sports/the-seoul-olympics-johnson-loses-gold-to-lewis-after-drug-test.html.

KOLLER, DIONNE. "An Olympic Antidoping Champion." *The New York Times*, 16 June 2016, www.nytimes.com/2016/06/16/opinion/an-olympic-antidoping-champion.html.

LONGMAN, JERÉ. "Did Flawed Data Lead Track Astray on Testosterone in Women?" *The New York Times*, 12 July 2018, www.nytimes.com/2018/07/12/sports/iaaf-caster-semenya.html.

MACUR, JULIET. "Armstrong's Wall of Silence Fell Rider by Rider." *The New York Times*, 20 Oct. 2012, www.nytimes.com/2012/10/21/sports/how-armstrongs-wall-fell-one-rider-at-a-time.html.

MACUR, JULIET. "End of the Ride for Lance Armstrong." *The New York Times*, 1 Mar. 2014, www.nytimes.com/2014/03/02/sports/cycling/end-of-the-ride-for-lance-armstrong.html.

MACUR, JULIET. "Enough. Give Russia Its Flag Back, Then Make Real Changes." *The New York Times*, 22 Feb. 2018, www.nytimes.com/2018/02/22/sports/olympics/russia-flag-doping.html.

MACUR, JULIET. "For Armstrong, a Confession Without Explanation." *The New York Times*, 18 Jan. 2013, www.nytimes.com/2013/01/18/sports/cycling/lance-armstrong-confesses-to-using-drugs-but-without-details.html.

MACUR, JULIET. "Gary Wadler, Antidoping Pioneer, Had a Gift for Straight

Talk." *The New York Times*, 13 Sept. 2017, www.nytimes.com/2017/09/13/sports/olympics/gary-wadler-wada-doping.html.

MACUR, JULIET. "Lance Armstrong Settles Federal Fraud Case for $5 Million." *The New York Times*, 19 Apr. 2018, www.nytimes.com/2018/04/19/sports/cycling/lance-armstrong-postal-service.html.

MCGOWEN, DEANE. "Doping Tests Urged for All Harness Horses Before Races at State Tracks." *The New York Times*, 13 Nov. 1959, timesmachine.nytimes.com/timesmachine/1959/11/13/89299132.pdf.

THE NEW YORK TIMES. "Dogs 'Doped' in Britain." *The New York Times*, 28 Feb. 1944, timesmachine.nytimes.com/timesmachine/1944/02/29/86847791.pdf.

THE NEW YORK TIMES. "Effect of Drugs to Aid Athletes Studied by U.S." *The New York Times*, 22 Aug. 1976, www.nytimes.com/1976/08/22/archives/effect-of-drugs-to-aid-athletes-studied-by-us-panel-of-us-olympic.html.

THE NEW YORK TIMES. "I.O.C. Issues Doping Report." *The New York Times*, 3 Aug. 1980, timesmachine.nytimes.com/timesmachine/1980/08/04/111268688.pdf.

THE NEW YORK TIMES. "Olympic Cover-Up?" *The New York Times*, 4 June 1989, www.nytimes.com/1989/06/04/sports/sports-people-olympic-cover-up.html.

THE NEW YORK TIMES. "U.S. Orders State Racing Bodies to Eliminate 'Doping' of Horses." *The New York Times*, 29 Mar. 1936, timesmachine.nytimes.com/timesmachine/1936/03/29/85270199.html.

O'CONNOR, ANAHAD. "A Better Body in a Pill? Experts Urge Caution on SARMs." *The New York Times*, 12 Apr. 2018, www.nytimes.com/2018/04/12/well/move/sarms-muscle-body-building-weight-lifting-pill-supplements-safety.html.

OKWONGA, MUSA. "Soccer and Doping? Don't Ask, Don't Tell." *The New York Times*, 26 June 2018, www.nytimes.com/2018/06/26/opinion/world-cup-soccer-fifa-doping.html.

PANJA, TARIQ. "Critics Say FIFA Is Stalling a Doping Inquiry as World Cup Nears." *The New York Times*, 3 Jan. 2018, www.nytimes.com/2018/01/03/sports/worldcup/world-cup-russia-doping.html.

PANJA, TARIQ. "Peru's Paolo Guerrero Vows to Fight Doping Ban: 'This Is About My Honor'." *The New York Times*, 18 May 2018, www.nytimes.com/2018/05/18/sports/soccer/peru-world-cup-paolo-guerrero.html.

POWELL, MICHAEL. "At the Heart of a Vast Doping Network, an Alias." *The New York Times*, 26 Mar. 2018, www.nytimes.com/2018/03/26/sports/doping-thomas-mann-peptides.html.

POWELL, MICHAEL. "The Home Run Explosion Is Not Exactly Beyond Suspicion." *The New York Times*, 22 Sept. 2017, www.nytimes.com/2017/09/21/sports/the-home-run-explosion-is-not-exactly-beyond-suspicion.html.

RHODEN, WILLIAM C. "Varying Standards on Steroid Use." *The New York Times*, 2 Oct. 1988, www.nytimes.com/1988/10/02/weekinreview/ideas-trends-varying-standards-on-steroid-use.html.

ROTHENBERG, BEN. "Madison Brengle Sues I.T.F. and WTA Over Injury From Blood Testing." *The New York Times*, 10 Apr. 2018, www.nytimes.com/2018/04/10/sports/tennis/madison-brengle-lawsuit-blood-testing.html.

RUIZ, REBECCA R. "Antidoping Authorities From 17 Nations Push for a Series of Reforms." *The New York Times*, 30 Aug. 2016, www.nytimes.com/2016/08/31/sports/antidoping-authorities-from-17-nations-push-for-a-series-of-reforms.html.

RUIZ, REBECCA R. "Antidoping Officials Get an Earful from Congress: 'What a Broken System'." *The New York Times*, 28 Feb. 2017, www.nytimes.com/2017/02/28/sports/antidoping-officials-get-an-earful-from-congress-what-a-broken-system.html.

RUIZ, REBECCA R. "Clashing Agendas: Antidoping Officials vs. U.S. Olympics Leaders." *The New York Times*, 27 Feb. 2017, www.nytimes.com/2017/02/27/sports/clashing-agendas-antidoping-officials-vs-us-olympics-leaders.html.

RUIZ, REBECCA R. "Drugs Pervade Sport in Russia, World Anti-Doping Agency Report Finds." *The New York Times*, 9 Nov. 2015, www.nytimes.com/2015/11/10/sports/russian-athletes-part-of-state-sponsored-doping-program-report-finds.html.

RUIZ, REBECCA R. "Russian Hackers Release Stolen Emails in New Effort to Undermine Doping Investigators." *The New York Times*, 10 Jan. 2018, www.nytimes.com/2018/01/10/sports/olympics/russian-hackers-emails-doping.html.

RUIZ, REBECCA R. "U.S. Lawmakers Seek to Criminalize Doping in Global Competitions." *The New York Times*, 12 June 2018, www.nytimes.com/2018/06/12/sports/american-doping-criminal-law.html.

RUIZ, REBECCA R., AND TARIQ PANJA. "Russia Banned From Winter Olympics by I.O.C." *The New York Times*, 5 Dec. 2017, www.nytimes.com/2017/12/05/sports/olympics/ioc-russia-winter-olympics.html.

RUIZ, REBECCA R., AND MICHAEL SCHWIRTZ. "Russian Insider Says State-Run Doping Fueled Olympic Gold." *The New York Times*, 12 May 2016, www.nytimes.com/2016/05/13/sports/russia-doping-sochi-olympics-2014.html.

WALDSTEIN, DAVID. "Exchanging Sword for Pen, Rodriguez Apologizes to Yankees and Fans." *The New York Times*, 17 Feb. 2015, www.nytimes.com/2015/02/18/sports/baseball/alex-rodriguez-apologizes-to-yankees-and-fans.html.

WALDSTEIN, DAVID. "Hall of Fame Voters Soften Stance on Stars of Steroids Era." *The New York Times*, 2 Jan. 2017, www.nytimes.com/2017/01/02/sports/baseball/hall-of-fame-steroids-baseball.html.

Index

Z

This book is current up until the time of printing. For the most up-to-date reporting, visit www.nytimes.com.